Cooking at the
KASBAH

Map
of the
TRACT of the CARAVANS,
Across SAHARA, from
FAS to TIMBUCTOO.

Cooking

20 15 10 5 0

Strait of Gibraltar

ALG

B A

EMPIRE of MAROCCO

Fas

Marocco

Atlas Mountains

Tafilelt

Bled el Je

Mogodor

C. de Geer

Agadeer

S.ta Cruz

SUS

Wad Noon for the accumulated

Caravans to Sodan

Tatta

Woled Deleim

Arabs

Dikna u Mjel

phundering Arabs

Soko Sea

Noon or Incon

C. Bajador

Woled Abbusebah

Jibbel Khal or

Black Mountains

Mograffra Arabs

East Tarassa

Ludaya Arabs A

Woled Abbusebah

H

A

Taudeny

C. Blanco

Arabs

S

Tejakant Arabs

Gum Forests

Arawa

West Tarassa Arabs

Brabee I.

Portandik

Senegal R.

Jinnie

Ni

C. Verd

BAMBAR

RECIPES FROM
MY MOROCCAN KITCHEN

at the KASBAH

KITTY MORSE

Food Photographs by Laurie Smith

Location Photographs by Owen Morse

CHRONICLE BOOKS

SAN FRANCISCO

Author's dedication

In memory of my father

Photographer's acknowledgments

The collaborative spirit among all who helped me to capture Kitty's beautiful food on film was extraordinary. The authenticity of the photographs would not have been possible without Kitty and Owen's gracious invitation to photograph at their home, using their precious collections from Morocco as props and having their invaluable guidance in helping me to get it just right. I give my heartfelt thanks to Kitty for her generous and cheerful offer to cook her very own food; to Owen for his enthusiastic and unparalleled role as jack-of-all-trades; to Deborah Madison for her vision and perfect sync as assistant, stylist, and friend; to Stella Long for her helping hands; to Laura Lovett and Chronicle Books for their belief in my photographic style; and as always, I embrace Bobby, Jamie, and Elizabeth for letting me be three wonderful things: a wife, a mother, and a photographer.

Library of Congress Cataloging-in-Publication Data:

Morse, Kitty
Cooking at the kasbah : recipes from my Moroccan kitchen / by
    Kitty Morse ; photographs by Laurie Smith
156 p.   20.4 x 23 cm.
Includes bibliographical references and index
ISBN 0-8118-1503-X (pbk.)
    1. Cookery, Moroccan. 2. Food habits—Morocco. I. Title.
TX725.M8M67   1998
641.5964—dc21   98-11490
                                           CIP

Text copyright © 1998 by Kitty Morse.

Photographs on pages 34, 37, 40, 46, 51, 54, 64, 70, 78, 83, 86, 90, 94, 102, 105, 110 117, 119, 124, 130, 134, 140, and 145 copyright © 1998 by Laurie Smith.

Photographs on pages 2, 5, 9, 10, 11, 13, 14, 17, 18, 21, 22, 23, 26, 27, 28, 29, 45, 69, 85 113, 115, and 129 copyright © 1998 by Owen Morse.

Manufactured in China

Designed by Stark Design

Distributed in Canada by Raincoast Books
9050 Shaughnessy Street
Vancouver, British Columbia V6P 6E5

10 9 8 7 6 5 4

Chronicle Books LLC
85 Second Street
San Francisco, California 94105

www.chroniclebooks.com

Contents

Preface

"... Kasbahs ... are the fortress-like enclosures which have long served as home and refuge, as defensive castles, villages and tribal domains of Berbers and Arabs. ..."
—from *The Kasbahs of Southern Morocco,* by Rom Landau

My father, Clive Chandler, arrived in Morocco as a young man, with the British Royal Air Force, in 1943. He fell in love with the country, with its people, and with its culture. He remained there for over half a century. In 1963, he purchased the ruins of a pasha's residence in Azemmour, inside the ramparts of the kasbah—the ancient walled quarter of the city. He and his wife, Hedda, with the help of local artisans, spent the next twenty years restoring the structure to its original Moorish splendor. They called it Dar Zitoun (House of the Olive) for the venerable wild olive tree that grew on the steep bank of the Oum er Rbia (Mother of Spring) river, which flowed peacefully past the graceful arched windows of the home's atrium.

Hassan-el-Wazzan, a Moorish geographer who later took the name Leo Africanus, mentions Azemmour and the Oum er Rbia in his *Description of Africa,* published in 1526. He tells how Portuguese colonists forced the kasbah's indigenous Berbers to pay tribute, in the form of thousands of pounds of *achabel,* a species of shad then plentiful in the river's estuary.

Portuguese domination of Azemmour was short-lived, partly due to the heroic efforts of brave Zemmouris like Sidi M'Herfi, "the hooded saint," as he was later known. He is believed to be buried under the main stairway of Dar Zitoun. Even today, pilgrims occasionally appear at our door seeking permission to pay their respects at his tomb.

However, it was another story I heard from Naïma Bounaïm, the granddaughter of the man who sold Dar Zitoun to my father, that proved so meaningful to me. According to Naïma, in the mid-1800s, the house belonged to Si Mohammed Ben Driss, a wealthy businessman from Tetouan, a city in northern Morocco steeped in Andalusian culture. He and his family were seduced by the charming quietude of the whitewashed Azemmour kasbah. Yet they longed for the refined cuisine of the more sophisticated Tetouan. They decided to open a cooking school in their home, hiring prominent Tetouanese cooks to train young Zemmouri women in the culinary arts.

This very unusual dragon motif exists only in the embroidery of Azemmour. It dates back to the eleventh century.

Naïma, who lived in the house until she was twelve, also recalls how, decades later, her great-aunt, Lalla Meryem, gave cooking lessons there. As a matter of fact, several of Lalla Meryem's former apprentices still cook professionally in the region. One of them, Lalla Lakhmar, introduced me to some wonderful Zemmouri specialties that I include in this book. She gave them to me orally, from memory, in the same way that recipes have been passed down in Morocco from generation to generation.

How strange that years before I knew the history of the house, I too would embark on a culinary career that would perpetuate the spirit of Lalla Meryem and her predecessors. And how extraordinary that I should come to test most of the recipes for my book at Dar Zitoun, in the same kitchen that they used. Join me now in this fragrant haven, which has been filled with the tantalizing aromas of mouthwatering creations for almost 150 years.

"Azemmour Protected by God"

Introduction ✺ Morocco.

The name itself invokes exotic images

of camel caravans and oases of palms set like verdant jewels in the vast Sahara. Many are surprised to learn that Al Maghreb Al Aksa ("the land where the sun sets") is primarily an agricultural nation, similar to California in climate and topography. The melting snows from the High Atlas Mountains feed the rivers and streams that nurture Morocco's fertile coastal plains and pre-Saharan oases.

Ancient Phoenician traders were well aware of the region's agricultural wealth. Over three thousand years ago, they traded their pottery, precious incense, and purple dye for the leopard skins, elephant tusks, and wine of the indigenous Berbers.

Beginning in the third century B.C., Carthaginian rulers laid claim to most of northwest Africa, including the land they called Maurusia. Their agricultural success and territorial expansion incurred the envy of the Romans, who wrested the area from Carthaginian control in the second century B.C. and renamed it Mauretania Tingitana. They further developed the cultivation of grapes, fruit, and olives. Wheat production also increased dramatically under Roman rule, supplying over 60 percent of the Empire's needs. Rome's domination of the region lasted almost five centuries. The indigenous Berbers adopted Roman language, religious practices, and social customs to such an extent that when Arab forces invaded the region in the seventh century A.D., they referred to the people as *roummi* (Romans).

The Arabs described their newly captured territory as "paradise," a land abounding with sheep and cattle, fields of grain, vineyards, and orchards of olive and fruit trees.

To this paradise they introduced the exotic flavors of Baghdad, Cairo, and Damascus, and spices like cinnamon, ginger, and peppercorns. In 711, the Moors (a word derived from Mauretania) crossed the Straits of Gibraltar to conquer Al Andalus (Spain). They would have an enormous influence on Spanish culture and the intellectual life of Western Europe for nearly eight centuries. In 1492, King Ferdinand and Queen Isabella recaptured Granada, the last city remaining under Moorish control. They gave the Islamic Moors and Sephardic Jews an ultimatum: Convert to Catholicism or be exiled.

Many sought refuge on Morocco's shores, settling mainly in the northern cities of Tetouan and Fez, which, to this day, remain proud centers of Andalusian culture. They introduced the art of making *ouarka*, the paper-thin dough used for b'stila. Some historians also credit them with developing the earliest recipes for couscous, now a staple of the Moroccan diet.

Chinese green tea, another staple of the Moroccan diet, was introduced by British merchants in the 1850s. Moroccans combined it with generous amounts of spearmint and sugar to create *atay b'nahna*, mint tea, the country's national drink.

Great Britain wasn't the only European nation interested in Morocco. France, Spain, Portugal, and Germany vied for control of the Moroccan market. In 1912, after years of political intrigue, France established the Protectorate and French settlers streamed into the country. Most of them were farmers who became known as *Pieds Noirs* (Black Feet) because of the black soil that clung to their boots. Following Moroccan independence in 1956, many Pieds Noirs returned to France, taking with them exotic recipes from Al Maghreb.

Today, American cooks are beginning to discover Moroccan cuisine. Magazines and newspapers in the United States regularly feature recipes for tagines and couscous, the durum-wheat semolina product sometimes marketed as "Moroccan pasta."

Moroccan cuisine is based on tradition. Recipes have always been transmitted orally, from mother to daughter. Yet today's *cuisinières* (cooks) understand the need to adapt time-honored recipes to the taste of an increasingly health-conscious population. As Boujemaa Mars, the executive chef at the famed La Mamounia Hotel in Marrakesh, told me: *"La cuisine traditionnelle, c'est délicieuse, mais de nos jours il faut savoir l'alléger!"* ("Traditional cuisine is delicious, but nowadays, you have to know how to make it lighter!") More and more cooks are experimenting with new ingredients. Chinese rice vermicelli, for instance, once found only in the country's Asian restaurants, are now a familiar item in big-city *marchés* (markets). I was surprised to discover them in a delicious seafood b'stila served in a popular Casablanca restaurant.

The flavors of Morocco have been a part of my life since childhood. I have shared meals with Berber families inside goat-hair tents in the Middle Atlas Mountains, and I have dined in the most exclusive restaurants of Marrakesh and Fez. I have also been fortunate to count among my family and friends in Morocco a number of superb cooks. From them, I acquired and adapted many of the recipes included in this book. I simplified and lightened when possible, taking great care to preserve the essence of the original dish. May some of these recipes find their way into your own repertoire of favorites.

Moroccan Cuisine

One of the highlights of the week for the residents of Azemmour is an expedition to the Tuesday souk. At this open-air market, a small army of itinerant vendors provides almost any product or service that the local people might need, from meat, spices, and fresh produce to clothing, dental extractions, haircuts, horseshoes, and jewelry for a dowry. The scene at Azemmour's weekly souk hasn't changed much since my maternal grandfather, Armand Darmon, a graduate of the Sorbonne's School of Oriental Languages and a French civil servant, arrived in Morocco at the beginning of the French Protectorate in 1913. In his memoirs he wrote:

"My first *souk* . . . what a colorful sight . . . bearded Arabs and Berbers dressed in their ample *burnous* . . .

and heavily laden camels, and asses, walking majestically by as their owners yelled out: *Balek!* [Make way!] . . . and fishermen with baskets filled with live fish on each arm, and over all, the smoke of grilling shish kabobs cooked right there on the grounds, mixed with the fragrance of fresh mint leaves. I was spellbound!"

As I approach the busy souk grounds, I am engulfed in the same flurry of commercial activity my grandfather described. The cornucopia from the surrounding Doukkala plain is on display all around me. I mingle with Zemmouri housewives and farmers from the countryside who push rickety carts weighed down with plump vine-ripened tomatoes, juicy lemons, and the deliciously sweet watermelons for which the Doukkala region is famous.

Recipes float through my mind while I survey the souk's seasonal offerings. I carefully inspect each item before handing it to the vendor for weighing. I press several coins into his weathered, outstretched hand to conclude our transaction. *"Chokran! Illalekah!"* ("Thank you! See you again soon!")

In another section of the bustling souk, large tents serve as grocery stores. A bevy of housewives engages in spirited bargaining for everything, from sugar loaves and olive oil to canned Moroccan sardines and small bottles of orange-flower water. Nearby, lively exchanges take place under the flimsy canopies sheltering the spice vendor and his neatly sculpted mounds of cumin, paprika, cinnamon, black pepper, and turmeric.

Dozens of cackling chickens nervously await their fate in makeshift coops lining one of the souk's dusty lanes. These free-range chickens are much sought after. So are the large brown eggs displayed on a bed of straw next to them. I carefully set a dozen fresh eggs inside my woven basket—just what I need for a mouth-watering egg tagine (see page 99).

The smoky aroma of brochettes grilling over charcoal braziers wafts through the air, and lures me to the area of the souk reserved for the meat vendors, where freshly slaughtered carcasses dangle from heavy metal hooks and large chunks of beef and lamb are displayed on beds of parsley.

I have just enough time to visit the fresh-herb vendor, partly hidden behind a mountain of mint. "Here, *Madame!* Smell this!" says the friendly, turbaned gentleman, handing me an aromatic sprig. I stuff several bunches of mint, cilantro, and green onions into my overflowing basket before heading back to my kitchen at Dar Zitoun.

THE DIFFA

"There were dishes of Kesksoo [couscous] set before us which seven men could hardly lift . . .

Water-melons, grapes, and other fruits were piled before us to sharpen appetite; drums and pipes sounded from daybreak to sunset. . . ." So wrote nineteenth-century British author John Drummond Hay describing an extravagant diffa he attended over 150 years ago.

Diffas, or feasts, are held on special occasions, like the anniversary of a local saint, a bountiful harvest, or a wedding. The last-named is, without a doubt, one of the most elaborate social and gastronomic events in Moroccan culture.

I was fortunate to be among the dozens of guests invited to a particularly memorable diffa celebrating the marriage of the daughter of an old family friend in Fez. I looked forward to the event with much anticipation, since Fez is known throughout Morocco for the refinement of its cuisine.

On the appointed day, I arrived at the massive front door of my hosts' sprawling villa. The

structure's thick walls could not stifle the joyous *youyous*, women's cries of celebration, that echoed from within. I was shown into the impressive carved-plaster foyer, where I kicked off my shoes before stepping onto the plush handwoven rugs that lined the floors of the enormous salon. I was welcomed with a glass of mint tea and a small silver plate of plump dates and dried almonds.

The demure young bride, dressed in a heavily brocaded kaftan, sat motionless on a carved wooden throne at the far end of the room, like a princess in a fairy tale. A crown of gold fili-gree held in place the diaphanous veil that covered her face. Her hands and feet were elabo-rately decorated with henna designs.

Men clad in white *djellabahs* and women in colorful kaftans of velvet and silk slowly filled the room. My host escorted me to one of the many low round tables, where I joined a handful of other guests. It was time for the feast to begin.

It started with the traditional hand-washing ceremony. A young servant poured warm water over my outstretched hands held above an ornate copper basin in the center of the table. I dried my hands to receive a few drops of orange-flower water, dispensed from a bulbous-shaped silver container called a *rashasha*. With great flourish, waiters in gold-trimmed black jackets circulated with baskets of warm anise-flavored bread called *hobz*.

"Bismillah!" invoked the celebrants in unison. Suddenly, an assortment of artistically gar-nished salads was set before me: roasted red peppers seasoned with cumin and olive oil, grated carrots lightly sprinkled with orange juice and cinnamon, and a tart mixture of minced cooked spinach, parsley, and garlic. I attacked them with gusto, using only a small piece of bread and the thumb and first two fingers of my right hand.

The waiters soon returned, this time bearing colorful ceramic platters that held crisp golden b'stilas, the quintessential Fez specialty. My diffa companions and I made short work of the exquisite blend of shredded chicken, cinnamon, sugar, and ground almonds nestled between layers of paper-thin ouarka dough.

A cloud of fragrant steam engulfed me as the waiter lifted the heavy conical lid from an earthenware platter containing a savory, mouth-watering tagine of chicken with preserved lemons and olives. Its exquisite flavor was perfectly counterbalanced by a tagine of lamb, prunes, and sesame seeds in an unctuous sauce of honey, ginger, and cinnamon.

The tagines were quickly carried off and replaced by an enormous platter of roast lamb. We pulled off succulent pieces of *mechoui*, as it is called, and dipped them into tiny saucers filled with ground cumin and salt.

"Here, this is for you," said the attentive gentleman seated to my right, as he handed me a particularly choice morsel.

Just when I thought I couldn't possibly eat another bite, I spied a steaming mountain of saffron-scented couscous garnished with meat and vegetables heading towards my table on the strong shoulders of a waiter. Following the lead of those around me, I fashioned small balls of couscous with my right hand and carefully propelled them into my mouth, using my thumb. Though I love couscous more than almost any other Moroccan dish, I knew I had reached my limit.

At least, I thought I had. The table was cleared once again to make room for glasses of sweet mint tea, bowls of fresh fruit, and a tray of honey-drenched briouats. I made a polite attempt to sample one or two pastries before surrendering. I fell back against the soft, plump pillows behind me and listened contentedly to the haunting melodies of the Andalusian orchestra playing outside on the jasmine-scented patio.

بِسْمِ اللهِ الرَّحْمَنِ الرَّحِيمِ

Bismillah! ("In the name of God")
The traditional Moroccan invocation at the beginning of a meal.

MOROCCAN HOSPITALITY

The solicitude with which Moroccans treat their guests is a long-held custom born of the nomadic lifestyle, which depends on the kindness of strangers in times of need. James Grey Jackson, a nineteenth-century British merchant and author who spent many years in Morocco, quotes one of his Moorish acquaintances:

"With us, a poor man may travel by public beneficence and apt hospitality from the shores of the Mediterranean to the borders of the Sahara without a fluce (small copper coin). . . . A traveller, however poor he may be, is never at a loss for a meal, several meals, and even for three days' entertainment wherever he travels through our country."

To satisfy the popular adage "First you eat with your eyes," the cooks of Al Maghreb take great care in the artful presentation of their dishes. Western guests in a Moroccan home are

often astonished by the lavishness of the meal set before them, yet leftovers never go to waste. The members of the host's extended family, not served with the guests, will see to that.

I have experienced such hospitality many times over the years. Once, while taking photographs of an ancient kasbah near Taliouine, Morocco's saffron-growing capital, I was approached by a bright-eyed little girl who had been watching me from a distance for some time. Her name was Jamiha. *"Breetee djee l'handee?"* ("Do you want to come to my house?"), she asked shyly. She took my hand and led me to the entrance of her family's modest white-washed adobe dwelling. Her parents were saffron farmers. Jamiha's mother Rabia greeted me warmly, and showed me to one of the brightly covered divans that lined the home's cool, narrow salon. Within minutes, one of Jamiha's younger sisters appeared holding a tray laden with an assortment of cookies, candies, almonds, and dates. Jamiha was right behind her, bearing the family's precious silver tea service, which she set before her mother. Rabia placed green tea and boiling water in the decorative teapot, then stuffed it with fresh mint, chunks of sugar loaf, and to my great surprise, an extravagant quantity of saffron. *"B'saha!"*

("To your health!") said Rabia, as she handed me a steaming glass of this unique local variation of Morocco's national drink.

Jamiha's family urged me to stay for dinner and spend the night. Unfortunately, my travel plans precluded me from accepting their gracious invitation. Later that evening, as I drove away from Taliouine, I detected a subtle, yet distinctive scent in the car. Someone had surreptitiously placed a small, tightly wrapped package of saffron on the seat next to me.

DINING ETIQUETTE

While silverware is increasingly common in Morocco, many traditional families use only the thumb and first two fingers of their right hand to pluck tender morsels from the communal dish. French anthropologist Louis Brunot explains this custom in his book, *Au Seuil de la vie marocaine:* "Formal manners dictate that one must only use three fingers to eat with—the thumb, forefinger, and middle finger; using only one finger bespeaks of the devil's influence; prophets eat with three; only gluttons eat with four or five. . . ."

The Moroccan Kitchen

Moroccan cooks rely on relatively few implements to create their exquisite dishes. Most women use a simple *canoun* (small charcoal brazier) as their only source of heat to boil water for mint tea, or to slow-cook a savory tagine. They also have at their disposal an assortment of earthenware platters with distinctive conical lids, called *tagine slaoui,* for making tagines, as well as several aluminum colander-capped soup pots called *keskess,* for making couscous. For grinding spices, they have a brass *mehraz,* or mortar and pestle. A shallow wooden or earthenware platter called a *ga'saa* is used for kneading dough, or rolling the semolina for couscous. Bread, as well as larger dishes like *mechoui,* or roast lamb, are taken to the public ovens for baking.

Wealthier households maintain two kitchens: one to prepare traditional dishes for special occasions, and another, more modern one, for everyday use. My friend Ahlam Lemseffer, a busy career woman in Casablanca, insists on cooking tagines and couscous on her charcoal *canoun* when she entertains. For her more mundane culinary activities, however, she prefers the convenience of a modern gas stove.

You don't have to own traditional implements to prepare good Moroccan food. An enameled casserole with a lid, a small Dutch oven, or a crockpot is a perfectly acceptable substitute for the traditional *tagine slaoui.* If a *keskess,* or *couscoussière,* for making couscous is not available, use a large stockpot or steamer topped with a tight-fitting colander or sieve. Line the bottom of the colander with a clean fine muslin dishcloth to prevent the couscous granules from slipping through the holes.

BASIC INGREDIENTS

Almond paste: A paste made of ground almonds and confectioners' sugar (and sometimes corn syrup or egg white), available in the baking section of many supermarkets. Some bakeries sell almond paste by the pound. To make your own, see page 136.

Barley grits: This hulless cracked barley, called *belboula* in Morocco, is used to make barley couscous. It has a coarser consistency and a nuttier flavor than regular couscous. You can find packages of instant barley grits in the cereal section of many natural foods stores, and in bulk in Middle Eastern markets.

Beans: Fava beans *(fool),* chickpeas (also called *ceci* beans, or garbanzo beans), and navy beans, all staples of the Moroccan diet, are available canned or dried in Middle Eastern markets and large supermarkets.

Couscous: This staple of the Moroccan diet is made from durum-wheat semolina mixed with smaller quantities of either durum-wheat flour or a soft-wheat flour, salt, and water. Couscous is available in bulk in Middle Eastern markets and in natural foods stores. Boxes of instant couscous are sold in the pasta and rice section of most supermarkets.

Cumin: Ground cumin seed is one of the most commonly used spices in Moroccan cuisine. Cumin seeds are usually lightly toasted to release their fragrance before being ground with a mortar and pestle.

Ginger, ground: An essential spice in Moroccan cooking. Fresh ginger is not used, however.

Green tea: Only Chinese green teas, such as young Hyson or Gunpowder, are used in the preparation of Moroccan mint tea. Do not substitute Japanese green tea. To order green teas, see Mail-Order Sources, page 150.

Harissa: This Tunisian hot sauce is now popular in Morocco. It is sometimes found in cans or in tubes in the specialty foods section of supermarkets, and in Middle Eastern markets. To make your own, see page 39.

Mint: Spearmint, the common backyard mint *(Mentha veridis),* is used to make mint tea.

Nuts: Almonds, walnuts, peanuts, and sometimes pine nuts are used in a number of Moroccan dishes.

Olives: Green, purple, and black olives are essential ingredients in Moroccan cuisine. The cultivation of olives dates back more than five thousand years. Phoenician traders introduced them to North Africa, although it wasn't until the Roman conquest of the region that their commercial cultivation became widespread.

The color of an olive depends on the stage at which it was harvested. Green olives have the firmest flesh, as they are first to be picked. As green olives mature, they turn purple, then black. Green and purple olives are sometimes cracked to allow for a better absorption of the flavorings, cured in water or brine, and combined with dried herbs, chilies, or preserved lemon. They are primarily used as appetizers, in salads, or as an ingredient in savory tagines. Sicilian olives or the diminutive picholines make good substitutes.

To store green olives, keep them covered in their brine in an airtight container in the refrigerator. Black olives, on the other hand, are generally dry- or salt-cured, like French Nyons or Greek Kalamata olives. These olives are generally served as appetizers, or used as a garnish for salads. To order, see Mail-Order Sources, page 150.

Olive oil: Most of the olive oil in Morocco is produced in Meknès and Moulay Idriss, mainly for the national market. Olive oil is an essential ingredient in Moroccan dishes, whether in raw or cooked salads, couscous, or tagines. Olive oil is extracted from the fruit of the olive tree by pressing, without the use of chemicals. Its flavor and quality varies according to climate, soil, amount of water, and environmental conditions at the time of harvest. Grades of olive oil differ in aroma, flavor, color, and level of acidity.

I prefer using extra-virgin olive oil, the fruitiest and highest grade of oil, in salad dressings, or when sautéing or browning foods. Research has shown that a diet high in mono-unsaturated fatty acids, like those found in olive oil, may help fight coronary heart disease by raising levels of HDL (the so-called good cholesterol). Keep olive oil in a tightly sealed container in a cool, dark place. You can also refrigerate olive oil. (Since the oil congeals, remember to bring it back to room temperature before use.)

Orange-flower water: Also called orange-blossom water. Distilled from the fragrant blossoms of the bitter-tasting Seville orange, it is used throughout the Maghreb to flavor pastries, desserts, and beverages. In the United States, orange-flower water is sold in some supermarkets and large liquor stores, as well as in Middle Eastern markets and specialty foods stores.

Paprika, sweet Hungarian: One of the most common spices in Moroccan cuisine. Do not substitute Mexican ground chili. To order sweet Hungarian paprika, see Mail-Order Sources, page 150.

Parsley: Flat-leaf parsley, sometimes marketed as Italian parsley in the United States, is used extensively in Morocco. Curly-leafed parsley may be substituted.

Phyllo dough: Sometimes spelled *filo*, this paper-thin Greek pastry dough is a good substitute for Moroccan ouarka. You can find phyllo dough in the frozen foods section of supermarkets. Fresh phyllo dough is also sold in some Greek markets in larger cities.

To thaw frozen phyllo, place it in the refrigerator overnight, or let it stand at room temperature for 2 hours. Frozen phyllo that has been thawed correctly should remain soft and pliable. When working with phyllo, keep it covered with a damp towel or plastic wrap; otherwise, it will dry out quickly and become brittle on exposure to air.

Rose water: Commercial rose water is obtained from the steam distillation of rose oil, primarily obtained from damask roses. In Morocco, rose water is distilled from the intensely fragrant roses cultivated in the pre-Saharan oasis of El-Kelaa M'Gouna. Rose water is sold in Middle Eastern markets, large supermarkets, and sometimes in pharmacies.

Saffron: Spanish saffron, the dried stigmas and part of the styles of the *Crocus sativus,* is the world's most expensive spice. It takes seventy-five thousand hand-picked crocus blossoms to obtain 1 pound. Saffron is cultivated commercially around Taliouine, a kasbah in southern Morocco. Moroccan cooks prefer to use saffron threads rather than saffron powder, as the latter is more easily adulterated with less-expensive spices. In Moroccan cooking, saffron is generally paired with turmeric powder to give sauces a rich orange-yellow tone.

To release saffron's intense aroma, place the desired number of threads in a small nonstick skillet and stir constantly over medium-high heat for 2 to 3 minutes. Crush the threads between your fingers, or pound them in a mortar along with a pinch of salt before using. Or, dilute the saffron in $1/4$ cup warm water or broth before adding it to your dish. Store saffron in a tightly sealed container in the refrigerator or freezer. Too much saffron will impart a bitter taste. Buyers beware: Stigmas of the considerably cheaper and relatively flavorless safflower are sometimes marketed as saffron. To order saffron, see Mail-Order Sources, page 150.

Sesame seeds: Used extensively in Moroccan breads and pastries, and often sprinkled over tagines as a garnish. Unhulled sesame seeds are a light golden color, in contrast to the hulled white variety. Either can be used.

Sun-dried tomatoes: Slices of tomatoes left to dry in the sun until they turn the consistency of soft leather acquire an intense tomato flavor. In Northern Morocco, sun-dried tomatoes are usually pounded into a paste with a little olive oil. Packages of commercial sun-dried tomatoes are available in most American supermarkets. To make your own, see page 43.

Turmeric: A rhizome that yields a yellowish-orange powder when dried and ground. It is often combined with saffron to enhance the color of Moroccan dishes.

BASIC TECHNIQUES

Peeling Fresh Fava Beans: After being shelled, small fava beans do not need to be peeled. Peeling is recommended for larger, more mature beans with their tougher skins. To peel these, make a small incision at the hilum (the small bump where the seed attaches to the pod) and squeeze between thumb and forefinger until the skin slips off.

Peeling and Seeding Tomatoes: In a saucepan of boiling water, blanch each tomato for 10 to 15 seconds. Remove with a slotted spoon and let cool. Peel and cut the tomatoes in half, gently squeezing out the seeds.

Roasting Peppers: You can grill peppers over charcoal, over an open flame, or under the broiler. For the broiler method, preheat the broiler. Place the peppers on a baking sheet or broiler pan. Broil, turning them with tongs and watching carefully, until the skin blisters and blackens, 10 to 12 minutes. Transfer the peppers to a plastic bag or a bowl and seal. Let stand until cool to the touch. Peel and seed.

Soaking Dried Beans: To soak dried chickpeas and kidney, fava, or navy beans, rinse and pick over the beans, then soak them overnight in a bowl of water to cover. Drain and proceed with the recipe. For the quick-soak method: Place 2 cups beans in a large soup pot and add 10 cups hot water and 1 bay leaf. Bring the water to a rolling boil for 3 minutes. Turn off the heat and let the beans soak for $1\frac{1}{2}$ to 2 hours. Drain the beans and proceed with the recipe. The older the beans, the longer they will take to cook.

Toasting Nuts: To toast on top of the stove: Put the nuts in a dry nonstick skillet over medium-high heat. Shake the pan back and forth, or stir with a wooden spoon, watching carefully until the nuts turn a light brown, 2 to 3 minutes. Remove the nuts from the pan and let cool.

To toast in the oven: Preheat the oven to 375 degrees F. Place the nuts on a baking sheet in a thin layer. Bake, stirring once or twice, until the nuts turn a light brown, about 5 to 8 minutes.

Toasting Saffron: Toasting saffron before use releases the precious spice's essential oils. For toasting and using saffron, see previous page.

Toasting Seeds: Pick over the seeds to remove any impurities. Heat a cast-iron or nonstick skillet over medium heat and toast the seeds, stirring constantly, until they begin to emit a more intense aroma. Set aside to cool. For a large amount of seeds, toast in the oven as for nuts, above.

L'KWAM

Basic Recipes

L'HAMD MARKAD
Preserved Lemons

Preserved lemons impart their distinctive flavor to a wide variety of dishes, from savory pastries to tagines and salads. There is no substitute for this unique Moroccan condiment. Because the lemons are preserved in salt, there should be no need for salting the dish in which they are used. In tagines, the softened rind generally is cut up and added at the end of the cooking process, while the jamlike pulp is blended with the sauce. Moroccan cooks favor thin-skinned Meyer lemons. Small thicker-skinned Eurekas also lend themselves well for this purpose. Allow at least 4 to 6 weeks to make preserved lemons.

Makes 1 quart

**12 or more unblemished, organically grown lemons,
preferably Meyers, scrubbed**

Sea salt

Fresh lemon juice as needed

Pat the lemons dry. Cut a thin dime-sized piece from both ends of each lemon. Set a lemon on one end and make a vertical cut three quarters of the way through the fruit, so that the two halves remain attached at the base; do not cut it in half. Turn the lemon upside down and make a second vertical cut at a 90-degree angle to the first, again three quarters of the way through the fruit. Fill each cut with as much salt as it will hold. Place the lemon carefully at the bottom of a sterilized wide-mouthed quart glass jar. Proceed in this manner with the remaining lemons, compressing them in the jar until no space is left and the lemon juice rises to the top. Seal and set aside on the kitchen counter.

More lemons may be added in the following days as the lemon rinds begin to soften. Make sure the lemons are covered with juice at all times, adding fresh lemon juice if necessary. The lemons are ready to use when the rinds are tender, in 4 to 6 weeks. Rinse them lightly and discard the seeds before using. Refrigerate after opening. Preserved lemons will keep for up to 6 months in the refrigerator.

Note: Mold may form when the lemons come in contact with the air. If this happens, remove the mold with a clean utensil. Be sure the lemons are always completely covered with lemon juice.

SMEN

Aged Butter

Smen, an aged butter similar to Asian ghee, is a prized flavoring ingredient in Moroccan dishes. Smen is made from clarified butter, dried herbs, and salt. It is aged in small earthenware pots in a cool, dry place until it acquires an aroma and consistency similar to Roquefort cheese. Berber farmers in southern Morocco bury a tightly sealed pot of smen on the day of a daughter's birth, unearthing it years later to flavor the couscous served on her wedding day. Berber tradition notwithstanding, I suggest you use the smen within six months. A teaspoon or two is usually all that is required to impart the characteristic taste to a dish of couscous or to the sauce of a tagine. You can substitute equal parts butter and olive oil in place of smen in a recipe, if you prefer.

Makes 1½ cups

1   pound unsalted butter
2   teaspoons dried oregano
1   tablespoon sea salt

In a medium saucepan, melt the butter over low heat. Wrap the oregano leaves in a square of cheesecloth and tie it closed with kitchen twine. Set the sachet in the butter. Simmer until the butter turns into a clear golden liquid and the white sediment settles on the bottom, 25 to 30 minutes. Skim off the foam. Discard the oregano sachet. Strain the butter through a clean fine muslin dish cloth once or twice until clear. Transfer to a hot sterilized wide-mouthed pint glass jar. Add the salt and mix well. Let stand in a cool place until the butter becomes pungent, 1 to 2 weeks. Refrigerate after opening. Use within 6 months.

HARISSA

North African Hot Sauce

The hot sauce called *harissa* is a staple of North African cuisine. The chilies from which it is made, however, were not indigenous to the region. The Spanish conquistadors introduced them to the Old World in the early 1500s upon their return from the Americas. In Tunisia, where harissa originated, the sauce is mixed liberally with almost every dish. Moroccans prefer to serve harissa on the side, adding it according to individual taste. You can make it as mild or as *picante* as you like, depending on the variety of chili peppers you use. For a milder harissa, use dried guajillo or ancho chilies. For a hotter harissa, substitute dried chipotles or pasilla chilies, and add one or two dried habaneros or Thai chilies. Remember to wear rubber gloves when working with chilies to avoid burning your hands. And don't touch your eyes!

Makes about 1 cup

12 **dried chilies**
4   **garlic cloves, minced**
½   **cup extra-virgin olive oil**
1   **teaspoon salt, or to taste**
1   **teaspoon ground cumin, or to taste**
Oil for topping

Wearing rubber gloves, open the chilies and remove the seeds. With scissors, cut the chilies into small pieces. Place in a bowl of warm water and soak until they soften, 25 to 30 minutes.

Squeeze the water from the chilies. Place them in a blender with the garlic, olive oil, salt, and cumin. Process until smooth. Transfer to a clean pint jar. Cover with a thin layer of oil. Use within 6 months.

Note: Commercial harissa is available in cans or tubes in some large supermarkets and Middle Eastern markets.

Basic Recipes

RAS EL HANOUT
Moroccan Spice Blend

There must be as many recipes for ras el hanout as there are spice vendors in Morocco. The name itself, which translates as "top (or head) of the shop," refers to the best combination of spices the seller can provide. Si Brahim, our spice vendor in Azemmour, incorporates thirty-four spices, dried roots, so-called aphrodisiacs, and other mysterious and unusual items. I prefer to use Naïma Lakhmar's more easily prepared, less elaborate recipe. She toasts all her ras el hanout ingredients before grinding. You can usually find blade mace, dried ginger root, and dried turmeric root in Middle Eastern markets. For a mail-order source see page 150.

Makes about ¼ cup

1   teaspoon allspice berries or 1¼ teaspoons ground allspice
1   whole nutmeg or 2 teaspoons ground nutmeg
20 threads Spanish saffron
2   teaspoons black peppercorns or 1½ teaspoons ground black pepper
1½ teaspoons blade mace (see Note) or ground mace
1   three-inch cinnamon stick or 1 teaspoon ground cinnamon
2   teaspoons cardamom seeds or 1½ teaspoons ground cardamom
2   two-inch pieces dried ginger or 2 teaspoons ground ginger
2   teaspoons salt
1   two-inch piece dried turmeric or 1 teaspoon ground

If using whole spices, put all the ingredients in a nonstick pan over medium-high heat and toast, stirring constantly, until the mixture emits a pleasant aroma, 3 to 5 minutes. Remove from heat and let cool. (This first step is not necessary if using commercially ground spices.) Using a mortar and pestle or a spice grinder, reduce the ingredients to a fine powder. Sift to remove fibrous elements. Place in a tightly sealed container and store in a cool, dark place, or in the freezer.

Note: Blade mace, also called mace blades, is the lacy, scarlet aril covering the nutmeg. It turns light brown as it dries. It is better known in its powdered form as ground mace.

left to right from top left: flat-leaf parsley, *merhaz* (mortar and pestle), cilantro, ground cumin, cinnamon sticks, packets of turmeric, saffron, ras el hanout (spice blend), sweet paprika, ground ginger

ZITOUN MESLALLA
Preserved Cracked Green Olives

Olives are one of the main staples of the Moroccan kitchen. They are often served at the beginning of a meal, or combined with beef, lamb, or chicken to create savory tagines. Moroccans are particularly fond of purple olives, picked as they turn from green to black, for tagines. For additional information on olives, see page 30. To order, see Mail-Order Sources, page 150.

Makes 1 pound

1   **pound fresh green olives**
Sea salt
¼ **Preserved Lemon (page 36), pulp removed, cut into strips**
1   **small dried red chili pepper (optional)**
½ **cup well-strained fresh lemon juice**
Olive oil for topping

On a clean surface, with a wooden mallet, lightly crack open the olives. Place them in a sterilized 1-quart glass jar and cover with cold water. Keep the olives submerged, using a small bowl or cup as a weight. Store in a cool place for 24 hours. Drain. In a separate container, make a brine by adding ¼ teaspoon salt to 1½ cups of water. Pour over the olives. Again keep them submerged with a small bowl or cup.

Change the brine every 2 days until the olives lose their bitter taste, 10 to 20 days. Try not to touch the olives with your fingers during the curing process, as this could contaminate them (see Note).

Drain and rinse the olives under cold running water and transfer to a sterilized 1-quart jar. Add the preserved lemon and the chili pepper, if desired. Set aside. In a saucepan, bring 1 cup water and the lemon juice to a boil. Dissolve 1 tablespoon sea salt in the liquid. Allow to cool and pour over the olives to within ½ inch of the top of the jar. Cover with a layer of olive oil and seal with a lid. Keep refrigerated. Leave the olives in this solution for 2 weeks before eating. They will keep for about 1 month from the time they are reopened.

Note: If at any time the olives turn soft and develop a foul or rancid odor, do not taste. Discard all the olives and start over.

Basic Recipes

MATISHA MIEB'SA
Sun-Dried Tomatoes

I was thrilled to discover that the process I follow for sun-drying tomatoes is also the one used by my friend Naïma Bounaïm of Casablanca. She acquired the method from her great-aunt, Lalla Meryem, who lived in Dar Zitoun before it came into our family. Naïma's great-aunt dried tomatoes in the full sun on the home's expansive terrace before preserving them in olive oil. When fresh tomatoes were out of season, she pounded her sun-dried substitutes into a thick and flavorful paste for use in tagines. I prefer to store my sun-dried tomatoes in self-sealing plastic bags in the freezer.

Makes 3 loosely packed cups (about 8 ounces)

8 pounds small, ripe tomatoes
Salt for sprinkling

Cut the tomatoes into $\frac{1}{4}$-inch slices. Set them on wire racks and place in full sun. Sprinkle lightly with salt. When they have dried on one side, turn the tomatoes over, and again sprinkle lightly with salt. Let dry for 2 or 3 days, or until the tomatoes feel like soft leather. Bring the tomatoes in at night, to avoid dampness. Place the dried tomatoes in self-sealing plastic bags and freeze for up to 6 months.

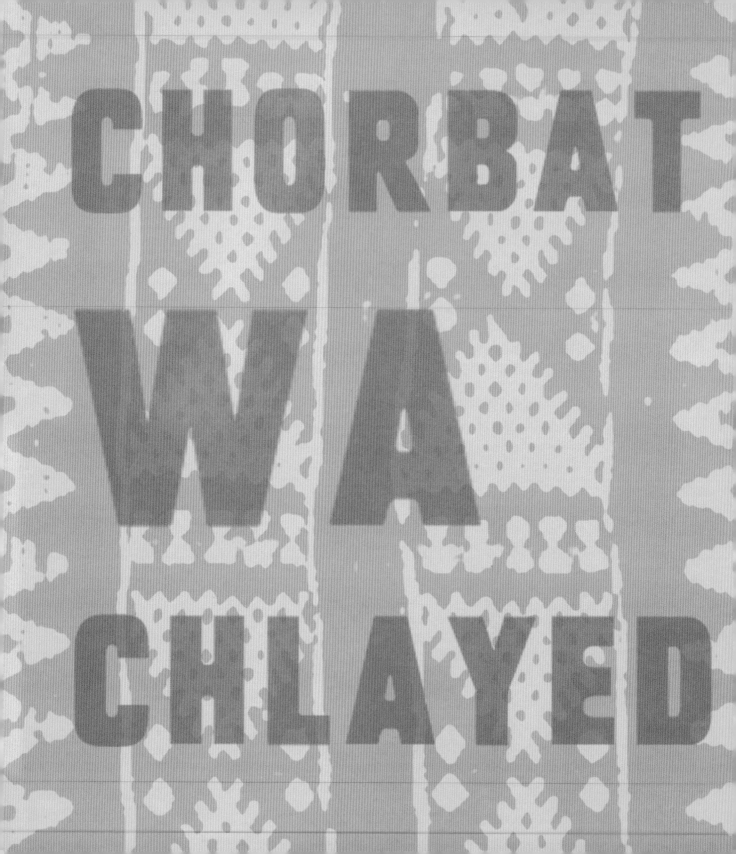

Soups and Salads

For centuries, Morocco's Arabs and Berbers have found shelter and protection in the fortified structures known as *kasbahs*, like the picturesque one that overlooks the oasis of Tinerhir, in the shadow of the High Atlas Mountains on the edge of the vast Sahara.

Melting snow feeds the icy stream that races through the Todra Gorge on its way to Tinerhir. Throughout the verdant oasis, Berber farmers quietly tend to their small, terraced plots. Occasionally, the soulful bray of a donkey or the muezzin's call to prayer disrupts the ambient serenity. In the relative cool of the late afternoon, colorfully clad women walk along the narrow earthen levees as they make their way from the communal well, balancing amphorae on their heads and adroitly side-stepping oncoming mules carrying fragrant cargoes of spearmint and fresh coriander. A bevy of chattering young girls crouches beside the gurgling *seguias,* or small irrigation channels, rinsing freshly harvested carrots, potatoes, and turnips.

Tradition and imagination guide Tinerhir's *cuisinières* (female cooks) in their use of the season's cornucopia. Lunch, the main meal of the day, often begins with an aromatic flotilla of saucers, each filled with a delectable salad: caramelized carrots in sweet paprika; a tart mixture of cooked spinach, preserved lemons, cilantro, and olives; and a refreshing blend of diced cucumbers and vine-ripened tomatoes, sprinkled with lemon juice and chopped spearmint—to mention just a few.

Unlike the more elaborate lunch, an evening meal in the oasis is less elaborate. Frequently, a small bowl of the *soup du jour* is served with a chunk of fresh bread called *hobz*. Often it will be *harira,* the most popular soup in Morocco, a sumptuous combination of tender cubes of lamb, garbanzo beans, lentils, tomatoes, garlic, and fresh coriander, simmered in a saffron and ginger-laced broth.

HARIRA
Ramadan Soup of Fava Beans and Lentils

Harira is the traditional soup served during the month-long observance of Ramadan. Each year, in the ninth month of the lunar calendar, devout Moslems everywhere must refrain from eating or drinking between sunrise and sunset. Moroccan families break each day's fast with a bowl of steaming harira, a handful of dates, and a coiled honey pastry known as *chebakiah*. Harira is usually thickened with *tedouira*, a mixture of flour, water, and yeast. I prefer to thicken my harira with crushed vermicelli, orzo, or the diminutive pasta called *acini di pepe*.

Serves 8

1   cup small, dried fava beans, soaked and drained (see page 33)

2   tablespoons olive oil

2   onions, finely diced

2   pounds lamb shoulder chops, cut into ½-inch cubes

8   Spanish saffron threads, toasted and crushed (see page 32)

1   teaspoon ground turmeric

2   teaspoons ground ginger

10 cups water

10 tomatoes (about 3 pounds), peeled, seeded, and coarsely chopped (see page 33)

30 fresh flat-leaf parsley sprigs, tied with cotton string

15 fresh cilantro sprigs, tied with cotton string

1   cup dried lentils, rinsed, picked free of impurities, and drained

1   teaspoon pepper

1   teaspoon ground cinnamon

½   cup crushed vermicelli, orzo, or acini di pepe

Salt to taste

Chopped fresh cilantro for garnish

Lemon wedges for serving

Skin the fava beans by squeezing each one between your thumb and forefinger. Set aside.

In a large soup pot over medium-high heat, heat the oil and sauté the onions and meat until the onions are tender, 4 to 5 minutes. Add the saffron, turmeric, ginger, and 8 cups of the water. Bring to a rolling boil. Cover, reduce heat to medium, and add the fava beans. Cover and cook until the beans are tender, 1 hour to 1½ hours (depending on the age of the beans).

In a blender or food processor, coarsely chop the tomatoes, parsley, and cilantro. Add the tomato mixture, lentils, pepper, and cinnamon to the beans. Cover and cook until the lentils are tender, 20 to 25 minutes.

In the meantime, bring the remaining 2 cups of water to a boil. Cook the pasta until tender, 6 to 8 minutes. Drain and add to the soup. Stir to blend. Season with salt. Heat through and ladle the soup into individual bowls. Top with fresh cilantro and serve immediately with wedges of lemon.

LOUBIA
Four-Spice Lamb and Bean Soup

Serves 6 to 8

Dried beans are an important part of the Moroccan diet. They are widely available and relatively inexpensive. This nourishing soup is usually reserved for the evening meal. Like most soups in the Moroccan repertoire, loubia is subject to each cook's interpretation.

3 onions

4 cloves

2 cups dried navy beans, soaked and drained (see page 33)

8 cups water

2 bay leaves

5 garlic cloves, minced

1 bone from a leg of lamb, or 1 pound lamb bones

2 tablespoons olive oil

6 tomatoes (about 2 pounds), peeled, seeded, and coarsely chopped (see page 33), or one 14¼-ounce can diced tomatoes

2 tablespoons tomato paste

2 teaspoons ground cumin

1 tablespoon sweet Hungarian paprika

⅛ teaspoon cayenne pepper (optional)

¼ cup fresh cilantro leaves

⅓ cup fresh flat-leaf parsley leaves

3 to 4 teaspoons salt

Freshly ground pepper to taste

Fresh cilantro leaves, chopped onion, and chopped green olives for garnish

Hobz Belboula (page 81) or pita bread for serving

Stud one of the onions with the cloves. In a soup pot, place the beans, water, bay leaves, clove-studded onion, garlic, and lamb bone(s). Cover and cook over medium heat until the beans are fairly tender, 1½ to 2 hours. Discard the onion.

Meanwhile, dice the 2 remaining onions. In a skillet over medium heat, heat the olive oil and sauté the onions until tender, 4 to 5 minutes. Add them to the beans, along with half the tomatoes, the tomato paste, cumin, paprika, and cayenne, if using.

In a blender or food processor, puree the remaining tomatoes with the cilantro and parsley. Add this mixture to the beans. Cover and cook until the meat is tender and the broth acquires a full-bodied flavor, 1 to 1½ hours. Season with salt and pepper. Ladle the soup into individual bowls and garnish with cilantro, onion, and olives. Serve with warm bread.

CHORBA DEL FOOL TREH

Passover Fava Bean Soup with Fresh Coriander

This is a soup for cilantro lovers. Following Sephardic tradition, Maman Darmon, my maternal great-grandmother, always made this soup for Passover. Fava beans, a staple of the Mediterranean diet, are among the world's oldest and most popular cultivated beans. In season, you can find fresh fava beans at farmers' markets and Middle Eastern and Italian grocery stores. Packages of frozen fava beans are sometimes available in Middle Eastern stores. You can also substitute frozen baby lima beans in this recipe, if you prefer.

Serves 6

1 pound beef chuck, cut into 1-inch cubes

1 large onion, coarsely diced

2 bay leaves

8 cups beef broth

1 turnip, peeled and quartered

1 potato, peeled and diced

2 pounds fresh fava beans, shelled, peeled if large (see page 33), or one 16-ounce package frozen baby lima beans

1 bunch fresh cilantro, stemmed

1½ teaspoons ground cumin

Salt and freshly ground pepper to taste

Harissa (page 39), for serving

In a large saucepan or soup pot, combine the beef, onion, bay leaves, broth, turnip, and potato. Cover and cook over medium heat until the meat is tender, 1 to 1½ hours. Discard the bay leaves. With a slotted spoon, transfer the meat to a bowl. Set aside. Add the beans to the broth and cook until tender, 10 to 15 minutes. Remove from the heat.

Reserve a few of the cilantro sprigs. In a blender or food processor, puree the vegetables, broth, and the remaining cilantro until smooth. Return the puree to the pan and add the meat. Season with cumin, salt, and pepper. Ladle the soup into individual bowls and garnish with the reserved cilantro sprigs. Serve with harissa on the side.

CHORBA B'HODRA
Saffron-Vegetable Soup

For a light supper, Moroccan families frequently enjoy this nourishing soup, several wedges of cumin-scented bread (see page 81), and a dessert of fresh fruit or yogurt. Chorba is sometimes thickened with a variety of large-grained couscous called *berkok* or *m'hammsa* (similar to the pasta product sometimes marketed as "Israeli couscous" in the United States), which is available mainly in Middle Eastern and some specialty foods markets. You may substitute crushed vermicelli, orzo, or acini di pepe.

Serves 6

2	tablespoons olive oil
½	onion, finely diced
1	pound beef or lamb stew meat, trimmed of fat and cut into ½-inch cubes
2	teaspoons sweet Hungarian paprika
8	fresh cilantro sprigs, tied with cotton string
12	fresh flat-leaf parsley sprigs, tied with cotton string
2	celery stalks with leaves, finely chopped
3	tomatoes, peeled, seeded, and coarsely chopped (see page 33)
1	potato, peeled and cut into ¼-inch dice

3	carrots, cut into ¼-inch dice
5	cups water
10	Spanish saffron threads, toasted and crushed (see page 32)
1	zucchini, cut into ¼-inch dice
¼	cup dried lentils, rinsed and drained
¼	cup crushed vermicelli, orzo, or acini di pepe
2	teaspoons salt
½	teaspoon pepper
	Chopped fresh flat-leaf parsley or cilantro leaves for garnish

In a large saucepan or soup pot over medium-high heat, heat the olive oil and sauté the onion, meat, and paprika until the onion is tender, 4 to 5 minutes. Add the cilantro, parsley, celery, tomatoes, potato, carrots, and water. Bring to a boil. Add the saffron. Cover and reduce heat to medium. Cook until the meat is tender, 45 to 50 minutes. Add the zucchini and lentils. Cover and cook until the lentils are tender, 20 to 25 minutes. Add the pasta, and cook until tender, 8 to 10 minutes. Discard the cilantro and parsley. Season with salt and pepper.

Ladle the soup into individual bowls, sprinkle with fresh parsley or cilantro, and serve.

CHLADA B'FELFLA WA L'HAMD MARKAD

Roasted Pepper, Preserved Lemon, and Parsley Salad

Serves 4

I love to serve this unusual, tangy salad as an accompaniment to grilled seafood. You can substitute a green bell pepper for the Anaheim chili, if you wish.

1 Anaheim chili, roasted, peeled, and seeded (see page 33)

3 lemons

¼ cup minced fresh flat-leaf parsley

2 garlic cloves, minced

¾ teaspoon salt

1 teaspoon ground cumin

1 tablespoon fresh lemon juice

2 tablespoons olive oil

2 teaspoons finely diced Preserved Lemon rind (page 36)

Finely dice the chili. Set aside. With a vegetable peeler or a paring knife, carefully remove the zest of 2 of the fresh lemons, taking care not to include the white pith. In a small saucepan filled with boiling water, blanch the zest for 2 minutes. Drain and let cool. Finely dice the zest and transfer it to a shallow bowl. Combine it with the chili, parsley, garlic, salt, cumin, lemon juice, olive oil, and preserved lemon rind. Set aside.

Cut the remaining lemon in half lengthwise. Cut each half crosswise into thin semicircular slices, discarding the seeds. To serve, heap the salad in the center of a small serving plate. Place the lemon slices in a scalloped pattern around the perimeter. Serve at room temperature.

HEZZU B'LIMMOUN

Diced Carrots with Cinnamon-Orange Dressing

Serves 4

This refreshing combination is traditionally made with grated carrots, but I prefer the crunchier texture of the diced vegetable. The addition of orange-flower water gives the dish its exotic flavor.

6   carrots, peeled and very finely diced

3   tablespoons fresh orange juice

1   tablespoon fresh lemon juice

Salt to taste

¼   teaspoon ground cinnamon

1   teaspoon minced fresh flat-leaf parsley

1   teaspoon orange-flower water (see page 31)

In a serving bowl, combine all the ingredients. Serve at once.

HEZZU M'CHERMEL
Caramelized Carrots with Sweet Paprika

The flavor of sweet, lightly caramelized carrots is wonderfully balanced by garlic and red wine vinegar in this classic Moroccan recipe. Like most Moroccan salads, this one tastes best when served at room temperature.

Serves 4

6   carrots, peeled and thinly sliced
3   garlic cloves, minced
1   teaspoon sweet Hungarian paprika
1   teaspoon sugar
¼   cup water
1   tablespoon red wine vinegar
Salt to taste
1   tablespoon minced fresh flat-leaf parsley for garnish

In a small saucepan, combine the carrots, garlic, paprika, sugar, and water. Cover and cook over medium-low heat until the carrots are lightly caramelized, 12 to 15 minutes. Add the vinegar and cook 1 minute longer. Remove from heat and season with salt. Let cool. Sprinkle with parsley and serve.

clockwise from top left: Minty Cucumber and Tomato Salad; Hearts of Romaine, Orange, and Date Salad; Grilled Three-Pepper Salad with Preserved Lemon; Caramelized Carrots with Sweet Paprika; Red Bell Pepper and Garlic Confit

MATISHA MHASSELA
Spiced Tomato and Honey Coulis

Makes about 2½ cups

This specialty comes from the Imperial City of Fez, the culinary capital of Morocco. The smooth mélange of cooked tomatoes, honey, and spices may be served on its own as a salad, or as a palate cleanser between the courses of a *diffa*, or feast. It is traditionally eaten with a spoon.

5 pounds tomatoes, peeled, seeded, and coarsely chopped (see page 33)
¾ teaspoon ground cinnamon
½ teaspoon ground ginger
¼ teaspoon pepper
2 tablespoons honey
¼ cup whole blanched almonds, toasted (see page 33)

In a large enameled pan, combine the tomatoes, cinnamon, and ginger. Partially cover and cook over low heat, stirring once or twice, until the mixture develops the consistency of a thick puree, 1 to 1 ½ hours. Add the pepper and honey. Cook, stirring, until the honey dissolves, 4 to 5 minutes. Transfer the mixture to a serving bowl. Garnish with the almonds and serve.

Note: This delicious puree will keep for up to 1 week in an airtight container in the refrigerator.

L'HASS B'LIMMOUN WA TMAR
Hearts of Romaine, Orange, and Date Salad

My friend Ahlam Lemseffer, a noted Moroccan artist, is also an excellent cook. She served this light and refreshing combination, along with several other delicious salads, as a prelude to an elegant Moroccan dinner she gave in my honor.

Serves 4

Tender inner leaves of 4 romaine lettuces

3   **sweet oranges**

½   **teaspoon ground cinnamon**

1   **tablespoon fresh lemon juice**

2   **teaspoons sugar, or to taste**

8   **dates, pitted and finely diced**

Cut the inner leaves of the lettuces into thin strips. Set aside. With a large, sharp knife, cut off the top and bottom of the oranges down to the flesh. Set the oranges on end and cut off the peel down to the flesh. Cut between each segment and the membrane on each side to release the segments. Remove any seeds. Squeeze the remaining connected membranes into a small bowl to yield about 3 tablespoons orange juice. Cut each segment into 2 or 3 pieces. Transfer the orange pieces to a bowl and sprinkle with the cinnamon. Set aside.

In a small bowl, whisk the lemon juice, orange juice, and sugar together. To serve, arrange equal portions of lettuce strips on 4 salad plates. Top with orange pieces and diced dates. Sprinkle with the dressing and serve immediately.

ZAHLOUK
Cooked Eggplant and Tomato Salad

Vegetable stands are so numerous along the narrow coastal road that runs between Casablanca and our home in Azemmour that I always add an extra hour to my travel time to allow for unscheduled stops. I carry one or two straw baskets in the trunk of my car, knowing from experience that somewhere en route I will be unable to resist the seasonal offerings, which might include crisp fennel bulbs, sweet mandarins, tender young asparagus, or wild morel mushrooms. On one trip, a cart laden with lustrous deep purple eggplants caught my eye: just what I needed to make *zahlouk*, Morocco's most ubiquitous salad, sometimes called "poor man's caviar."

Serves 4

1   firm globe eggplant (about 1 pound)
2   tablespoons olive oil
4   ripe tomatoes, peeled, seeded, and coarsely chopped (see page 33)
½   teaspoon sweet Hungarian paprika
1   teaspoon ground cumin
4   garlic cloves, minced
2   tablespoons minced fresh flat-leaf parsley
2   tablespoons minced fresh cilantro
Salt and freshly ground pepper to taste
1   tablespoon fresh lemon juice
Fresh flat-leaf parsley leaves for garnish

Preheat the oven to 375 degrees F. Prick the eggplant in several places with a fork and set it in a small baking pan. Bake it until tender, 50 minutes to 1 hour. Remove the eggplant from the oven and let it cool. Using a spoon, scoop out the flesh. Set aside.

In a medium, heavy saucepan or skillet over medium heat, heat the oil and cook the tomatoes, stirring occasionally, for 5 to 6 minutes. Add the eggplant, paprika, cumin, garlic, parsley, and cilantro. Reduce heat to low. Cover and cook, stirring occasionally, until most of the liquid evaporates, 20 to 25 minutes. Season with salt and pepper. Transfer the salad to a serving dish and stir in the lemon juice. Garnish with parsley leaves. Serve at room temperature.

BOKKOLA B'ZITOUN
Chopped Spinach Salad with Preserved Lemons and Olives

Serves 4

This recipe made a spinach-lover out of my husband. You will need to prepare the preserved lemons several weeks ahead of time. Black olives are not recommended for this dish.

2   bunches (about 1½ pounds) fresh spinach, stemmed and washed

2   tablespoons olive oil

1   tablespoon sweet Hungarian paprika

1   tablespoon ground cumin

1   teaspoon pepper

6   tablespoons minced fresh cilantro

3   garlic cloves, minced

15 green olives, pitted

2   teaspoons finely diced Preserved Lemon rind (page 36)

1   small lemon, cut into thin slices

In a large pot of boiling water, blanch the spinach until it wilts, 2 to 3 minutes. Drain in a colander. When it is cool enough to handle, press the spinach with the back of a large spoon to remove excess water. On a cutting board, chop the spinach finely and set aside.

In a large skillet over medium heat, combine the olive oil, paprika, cumin, and black pepper. Cook, stirring constantly, 1 to 2 minutes. Add the chopped spinach, cilantro, and garlic, and cook, stirring constantly, until most of the liquid evaporates, 8 to 10 minutes.

Reserve 6 of the olives. Finely chop the remaining olives. Combine the chopped olives and the diced preserved lemon with the spinach. Cook until heated through, 2 to 3 minutes. Set aside to cool.

To serve, mound the spinach in the center of a serving plate. Dot the salad with the reserved olives. Cut the lemon slices in half and place them around the plate to create a scalloped border. Serve at room temperature.

FELFLA HAMRA M'KLIYA
Red Bell Pepper and Garlic Confit

Every year, I look forward to the arrival of colorful red bell peppers to make this ambrosial con-fit. I first had it at the home of a friend in Fez. I noticed a twinkle in her eye as she placed the dish before me, already knowing what my reaction would be. I could have made a whole meal out of this delicious confit! Do not substitute green or yellow peppers in this recipe.

Serves 4

5   red bell peppers (about 2 pounds), roasted, peeled, and seeded (see page 33)
Salt for sprinkling
3   tablespoons extra-virgin olive oil
2   garlic cloves, minced

Cut the roasted peppers into 1-inch strips and sprinkle them lightly with salt. Place them in a colander and drain in the refrigerator for at least 4 hours or overnight.

In a large skillet over medium-low heat, heat the olive oil and sauté the garlic until golden, 1 to 2 minutes. Add the roasted pepper strips and fry gently for 3 to 4 minutes on each side. Using a slotted spoon, transfer the peppers and garlic to paper towels to drain. Transfer to a small bowl. Serve at room temperature.

MESLALLA
Orange and Olive Salad

Moroccans, like most Mediterraneans, consume large quantities of olives. At the colorful olive market in the Casablanca medina, or old city, large blue barrels overflow with glistening mounds of green, purple, and black olives. Some are flavored with fiery red chilies, others with preserved lemons, garlic, or sour Seville oranges, like the ones I frequently use for this dish. You can also make this with blood oranges, sweet Valencias, or navels. For a source of Moroccan olives, see Mail-Order Sources, page 150.

Serves 4

4   oranges
20   black olives, pitted and coarsely chopped
½   teaspoon ground cumin
¼   teaspoon sweet Hungarian paprika
Lettuce leaves for serving
Minced fresh flat-leaf parsley for garnish

With a large, sharp knife, cut off the top and bottom of the oranges down to the flesh. Set the oranges on end and cut off the peel down to the flesh. Cut between the membranes on each side of the segments to release the segments. Remove any seeds. Cut each segment into 3 pieces. In a medium bowl, combine them with the olives, cumin, and paprika. Mix to blend. Line a medium bowl with lettuce leaves. Top with the orange salad. Garnish with parsley and serve.

CHLADA B'FOOL WA ZITOUN
Fresh Fava Bean and Olive Salad

Serves 4

Fava beans make their appearance in early spring. Here, they are combined with green olives and cilantro to make a verdant spring salad.

1 tablespoon olive oil

1 pound fresh fava beans, shelled, peeled if large (see page 33)

¼ cup water

3 garlic cloves

1 teaspoon sweet Hungarian paprika

12 green olives, pitted, rinsed, and drained

1 tablespoon fresh lemon juice

1 teaspoon finely diced Preserved Lemon rind (page 36)

2 tablespoons minced fresh cilantro

In a medium saucepan, combine the olive oil, fava beans, water, garlic, and paprika. Cover and cook over medium heat until the beans are tender, 10 to 15 minutes. Add the olives, lemon juice, and lemon rind. Cook, stirring constantly, for 1 or 2 minutes. Transfer to a serving bowl and add the cilantro. Serve warm or at room temperature.

BISSARA
Fresh Fava Bean Dip

Every man believes that his fava beans are the best —Moroccan Saying

This is my adaptation of *bissara,* a traditional puree of dried fava or garbanzo beans, similar to Middle Eastern hummus. I like to make this delightful alternative with the fresh fava beans that make their annual appearance in early spring. Once shelled, small, tender young fava beans do not need to be peeled.

Makes about 2 cups

2   **pounds fresh fava beans, shelled, peeled if large (see page 33)**
3   **tablespoons fresh lemon juice**
5   **tablespoons extra-virgin olive oil**
¼   **teaspoon salt**
½   **teaspoon ground cumin**
2   **teaspoons minced fresh flat-leaf parsley**
Pita bread wedges, sliced raw vegetables, or crackers for serving

Fill a medium saucepan with water and bring it to a boil. Blanch the beans for 2 or 3 minutes. Drain, reserving 3 tablespoons of the cooking liquid. Peel if the beans are large.

In a blender or food processor, combine half the beans, the reserved liquid, and the lemon juice. (Add more liquid if you prefer a thinner dip.) Process, scraping down the sides with a spatula, until the mixture is fairly smooth. Add the remaining beans and the oil, and process until smooth. Transfer to a serving bowl and stir in the salt and cumin. Sprinkle with the parsley. Serve with pita bread, vegetables, or crackers for dipping.

CHLADA FELFLA MECHWIYA

Grilled Three-Pepper Salad
with Preserved Lemon

Serves 4

For me, the sweet smell of peppers grilling over a charcoal brazier is one of the most evocative aromas of Moroccan cooking. Combine red, yellow, and green bell peppers for a colorful salad.

3   large bell peppers, roasted, peeled, and seeded (see page 33)
2   garlic cloves, minced
2   tablespoons olive oil
1   teaspoon ground cumin
½   teaspoon salt
¼   teaspoon pepper
2   tablespoons fresh lemon juice
1   tablespoon minced fresh flat-leaf parsley
2   teaspoons diced Preserved Lemon rind (page 36)
1   twist of lemon peel for garnish

Finely dice the roasted peppers and set them in a colander to drain for 30 minutes to 1 hour. In a serving bowl, combine the peppers, garlic, olive oil, cumin, salt, pepper, lemon juice, parsley, and preserved lemon rind. Garnish with the fresh lemon peel. Serve at room temperature.

SEBHA DEL HDAREE
Ratatouille with Dates

Eggplants were introduced to Morocco during the Arab conquest of North Africa in the late seventh century. They have been an important ingredient in Moroccan cuisine ever since, used in everything from salads to tagines. Dates give this eggplant ratatouille a sweet North African accent.

Serves 6 to 8

4	tablespoons olive oil
1	onion, chopped
1	red bell pepper, seeded, deribbed, and diced
3	tomatoes, coarsely chopped
1	fresh rosemary sprig
1	bay leaf
4	garlic cloves, minced

1	eggplant, peeled and cubed
2	zucchini, cubed
½	cup dates, pitted and chopped
2	teaspoons sweet Hungarian paprika
	Salt and freshly ground pepper to taste
2	tablespoons slivered almonds, toasted (see page 33)

Preheat the oven to 375 degrees F. In a medium enameled casserole over medium-high heat, heat 2 tablespoons of the olive oil and sauté the onion and the pepper until tender, 3 to 4 minutes. Add the tomatoes, rosemary, bay leaf, and garlic. Set aside.

Meanwhile, in a medium skillet over medium heat, heat the remaining 2 tablespoons olive oil and cook the eggplant and zucchini until the zucchini are golden, 3 to 4 minutes. Drain on paper towels. Add the eggplant, zucchini, dates, and paprika to the mixture in the casserole. Stir to blend.

Cover tightly and bake until the vegetables are tender, 25 to 30 minutes. Remove from the oven and discard the rosemary and the bay leaf. Season with salt and pepper. Garnish with toasted almonds. Serve hot or at room temperature.

FEKKOUS WA MATISHA B'NAHNA
Minty Cucumber and Tomato Salad

Mint leaves add a wonderfully refreshing note to this classic Moroccan salad made with the slender cucumbers called *fekkous,* which are sometimes marketed as English, European, or hothouse cucumbers in the United States.

Serves 4

1   large seedless cucumber, peeled and finely chopped
2   ripe tomatoes, peeled, seeded, and chopped (see page 33)
2   green onions, green tops included, finely chopped
1   tablespoon minced fresh mint
2   tablespoons olive oil
2   teaspoons fresh lemon juice
Salt and freshly ground pepper to taste
Fresh mint leaves for garnish

In a serving bowl, combine the cucumber, tomatoes, onions, mint, olive oil, lemon juice, salt, and pepper. Garnish with mint leaves. Serve at room temperature.

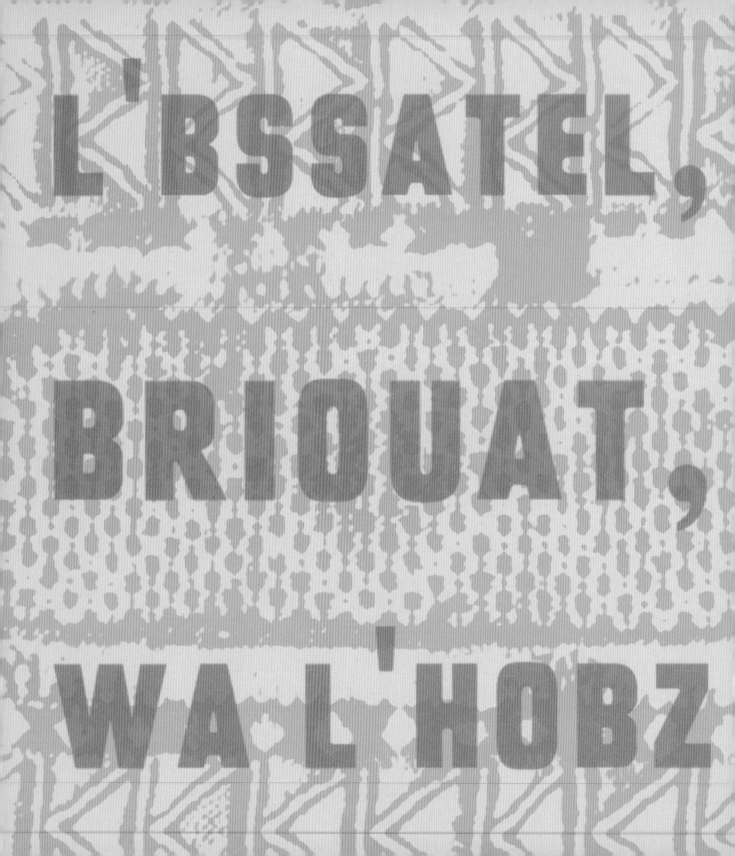

L'BSSATEL,

BRIOUAT,

WA L'HOBZ

Savory Pastries and Breads

B'stila is widely regarded as the crowning dish of Moroccan cuisine. In Fez, the country's culinary capital, this delightful pastry is traditionally served to newlyweds the morning after their wedding night to symbolize their family's wish that their life together be as sweet as this sublime creation. The origin of b'stila remains the subject of debate among food historians. Some believe it was created by the Persians and adopted by their Arab neighbors, who popularized it during the conquest of North Africa. Other experts argue that credit for the dish must go to the innovative cooks of Al Andalus, the medieval Arabic name for Spain. Whatever its origin, today b'stila is firmly established as a quintessentially Moroccan specialty.

B'stila was traditionally made with pigeon, although nowadays chicken is more commonly used. The meat is simmered in a sauce redolent of saffron, cinnamon, and ground ginger, then shredded and mixed with scrambled eggs, ground almonds, and powdered sugar to form an exquisite filling that is layered between sheets of a paper-thin phyllolike dough called *ouarka*.

A golden b'stila, just out of the oven, garnished with powdered sugar and decorated with cinnamon, never fails to elicit appreciative exclamations from around the table. A solicitous Moroccan host will quickly poke several holes in the flaky outer crust to allow some of the trapped fragrant steam to escape. He invokes the blessing *"Bismillah!"* before deftly breaking off a tasty morsel and offering it to one of his honored guests.

B'STILA B'DJEJ
Chicken B'stila

Makes one
10-inch
pastry

B'stila calls for a paper-thin pastry dough called *ouarka,* whose preparation is an art requiring considerable expertise. In Morocco, it is mainly the domain of the *dadas,* women descended from Sudanese slaves. They are reputed for their skill at creating the translucent round leaves. These ouarka specialists sit by the hour in front of a small charcoal fire, dexterously dabbing a ball of moist, slippery dough on the hot tin-plated outside surface of a round copper pan (much like a modern upside-down crepe griddle) called *tabsil dial ouarka* that rests just above the glowing coals. The *tabsil* is evenly covered with overlapping circles of dough. Within a minute, a leaf of translucent ouarka as thin as onion skin is deftly peeled from the pan. Most modern Moroccan housewives purchase ready-made ouarka at their local market. Phyllo dough makes an excellent substitute for ouarka.

Filling:

2   tablespoons vegetable oil

1   onion, finely chopped

6   skinned chicken thighs

3   boneless, skinless chicken breast halves

¼   cup minced fresh flat-leaf parsley

2   tablespoons minced fresh cilantro

¼   teaspoon ground turmeric

8   threads Spanish saffron, toasted and crushed (see page 32)

1   cup water

1   teaspoon ground ginger

1¼ teaspoons ground cinnamon

3   eggs, lightly beaten

1   teaspoon salt

½   teaspoon pepper

⅔   cup powdered sugar

Almond Mixture:

½   cup whole blanched almonds

½   cup powdered sugar

1   teaspoon ground cinnamon

12 sheets phyllo dough, thawed

1   cup (2 sticks) butter, melted

Ground cinnamon and powdered sugar for garnish

To make the filling: In a large enameled saucepan or a small Dutch oven over medium heat, heat the oil. Sauté the onion until golden, 6 to 8 minutes. Add the chicken, parsley, cilantro, turmeric, saffron, water, ginger, and cinnamon. Cover and cook until the chicken is tender, 20 to 25 minutes. With a slotted spoon, transfer the chicken to a bowl and set aside to cool.

Let the sauce continue to simmer in the pan and add the beaten eggs, salt, pepper, and

(continued)

sugar. Stir constantly until the eggs are scrambled. Bone and shred the chicken and add it to the eggs. Set aside.

To make the almond mixture: In a blender or food processor, coarsely grind the almonds. Transfer them to a small bowl and mix them with the sugar and cinnamon. Set aside.

Preheat the oven to 425 degrees F. Remove 12 sheets of phyllo from the package and rewrap the remaining phyllo in its original plastic wrap. Refrigerate for another use.

Stack the 12 sheets on a work surface. Using a sharp knife, with a 12-inch pizza pan as a template, cut through the stacked phyllo sheets. Discard the scraps. With a pastry brush, paint the pizza pan with a little melted butter. Keep the phyllo leaves covered with a damp cloth as you work.

Layer 3 round phyllo leaves on the pan, lightly brushing each with melted butter. Sprinkle the third leaf lightly and evenly with the almond mixture. Layer and butter 3 more leaves. Spread the chicken mixture evenly over the top, leaving a 1 1/2-inch border of phyllo. Fold over the edges to partially cover the chicken mixture. Layer and butter 3 more leaves over the chicken, sprinkling the remaining ground almond mixture evenly over the top. Layer and butter the last 3 leaves of phyllo over the almond mixture. Tuck the edges of these last 6 leaves under the b'stila as you would a bed sheet.

Bake the b'stila until golden brown, 20 to 25 minutes. Place the powdered sugar in a fine-meshed sieve. Tap the sides of the sieve to cover the surface of the b'stila lightly and evenly with sugar. Using your thumb and forefinger, sprinkle ground cinnamon in 6 or 8 intersecting lines to create a diamond-shaped pattern, or use a paper doily or template to make your own individual design. Serve immediately, before the pastry becomes soggy.

Note: I often prepare several b'stilas at a time, baking and serving one while freezing the others uncooked wrapped in aluminum foil. They will keep for up to 2 months in the freezer. There is no need to thaw a frozen b'stila before baking, but it will require about 10 more minutes in the oven.

KRAIYCHLET
Anise and Sesame Seed Buns

Sunday mornings in Azemmour find me seated in front of the large arched window in our atrium at Dar Zitoun, leisurely dunking one of these delicious kraiychlet buns into a steaming cup of *café au lait*. I watch the activity on the opposite side of the Oum er Rbia river, where horse-drawn wagons shuttle excited groups of young women to the centuries-old shrine of Lalla Aïcha Bahria (Lalla Aïcha by-the-Sea), two miles down the dirt road that leads to the Atlantic. They come from all parts of the country hoping to receive *baraka* (benediction) from the holy woman's spirit in order to resolve their affairs of the heart.

Makes about 20 buns

½ cup warm (105 to 115 degrees F) milk
1 package active dry yeast
¼ cup aniseed, toasted (see page 33)
⅓ cup sesame seeds, toasted (see page 33)
4 eggs
¼ teaspoon salt

½ cup sugar
⅓ cup orange-flower water (see page 31)
½ cup plus 2 tablespoons water
⅓ cup vegetable oil
⅓ cup (⅔ stick) butter, melted
5¼ to 5½ cups bread flour

In a small bowl, combine the warm milk and yeast. Set aside until foamy, about 10 minutes. Meanwhile, coarsely grind the aniseed with a mortar and pestle or a spice grinder. Set aside.

Reserve 1 tablespoon of sesame seeds. In a large bowl, lightly beat 2 of the eggs with the remaining sesame seeds, the aniseed, salt, sugar, orange-flower water, the ½ cup water, the oil, and butter. Stir well. Add 3 cups of the flour and stir to blend. Make a well in the center and stir in the yeast mixture and the remaining flour. When the dough becomes too difficult to stir with a spoon, turn it out onto a lightly floured board. Knead until it is smooth and elastic, 8 to 10 minutes. Shape it into a large ball and let it rest for 15 to 20 minutes.

Pinch off pieces of dough each about the size of an egg. Roll each one into a small ball between the palms of your hands. Place the balls on a lightly floured nonstick baking sheet, flattening each to about 4 inches in diameter. Cover with a clean towel. Set aside to rise in a warm (about 75 degrees F) place, away from drafts, until almost doubled in size, 20 to 30 minutes.

Preheat the oven to 350 degrees F. In a small bowl, lightly beat the 2 remaining eggs with the 2 tablespoons water. Brush the rolls with the egg wash. Prick each roll in several places with a toothpick. Sprinkle each roll with a little sesame seeds. Bake until golden brown, 10 to 12 minutes. Let cool on a rack.

B'STILA B'HOOT
Seafood B'stila with Tomato-Chermoula Sauce

Makes one 10-inch b'stila

In recent years, I have discovered a number of untraditional yet delicious fillings for b'stila. This savory seafood variation is one of them. I like to accompany the b'stila with a tomato sauce flavored with the aromatic blend of cumin, paprika, garlic, and cilantro used in the marinade called chermoula. Seafood b'stila is ideal as the first course for an elegant dinner, or as the main course for a light lunch. You can use any firm-fleshed fish, like mahimahi, red snapper, sea bass, or orange roughy. For Moroccan green olives, see Mail-Order Sources, page 150.

Filling:

2 tablespoons olive oil

2 onions, very finely diced

1 garlic clove, minced

2 tomatoes, seeded and diced

2 teaspoons sweet Hungarian paprika

2 teaspoons ground cumin

15 green olives, pitted, drained, and finely chopped

3 tablespoons fresh lemon juice

3 four-ounce boned firm white fish fillets, cut into 1-inch pieces

¾ teaspoon salt

2 tablespoons minced fresh cilantro

3 tablespoons minced fresh flat-leaf parsley

⅛ teaspoon cayenne pepper (optional)

Tomato-Chermoula Sauce:

2 tablespoons olive oil

2 garlic cloves, minced

1 teaspoon ground cumin

2 teaspoons sweet Hungarian paprika

5 tomatoes, peeled, seeded, and coarsely chopped (see page 33)

¼ teaspoon sugar

3 tablespoons minced fresh flat-leaf parsley

2 tablespoons minced fresh cilantro sprigs

½ teaspoon salt

8 sheets phyllo dough, thawed

½ cup (1 stick) butter, melted

To make the filling: In a large skillet over medium-high heat, heat the olive oil and cook the onions and garlic, stirring occasionally, until the onions are tender, 5 to 6 minutes. Add the tomatoes, paprika, cumin, olives, and lemon juice. Cook, stirring, for 1 minute. Add the fish, and cook, stirring, until it begins to flake, 6 to 8 minutes. Remove from heat and shred the fish. Combine it with the salt, cilantro, parsley, and cayenne, if using. Set aside to cool.

To make the sauce: In a medium saucepan over medium heat, cook and stir the olive oil, garlic, cumin, and paprika until fragrant, 2 to 3 minutes. Add the tomatoes, sugar, parsley, and cilantro. Cook, stirring occasionally, until the sauce thickens slightly, 8 to 10 minutes. Season with salt. Set aside and keep warm.

Preheat the oven to 425 degrees F. Remove 8 sheets from the package of phyllo and rewrap the remaining phyllo. Refrigerate for another use.

Set the 8 stacked sheets on a work surface. Using a sharp knife, with a 12-inch pizza pan as a template, cut through the stack of phyllo sheets. Discard the scraps. With a pastry brush, paint the pizza pan with a little melted butter.

Layer 4 round phyllo leaves on the pan, brushing each one lightly with melted butter. Spread the seafood mixture evenly over the fourth leaf, leaving a 1½-inch border of phyllo. Fold over the edges to partially cover the filling. Layer and butter the remaining 4 leaves of phyllo over the seafood and tuck them under the b'stila as you would a bed sheet.

Bake the b'stila until golden brown, 20 to 25 minutes. Cut the b'stila in wedges and serve *immediately* with the warm sauce on the side.

BRIOUAT B'KEFTA
Beef and Lamb Briouats

Makes about 2 dozen briouats

The word *brioaut* means "small letter" in Arabic, no doubt because of the envelopelike appearance of these folded phyllo pastries (although some Moroccan cooks I know prefer to make them in the shape of a Chinese egg roll). In briouats, as in b'stilas, ouarka encloses a variety of either sweet or savory fillings.

Filling:

8   ounces twice-ground beef

8   ounces twice-ground lamb

½   onion, finely diced

2   garlic cloves, minced

1   tablespoon minced fresh mint

2   tablespoons minced fresh flat-leaf parsley

1   teaspoon sweet Hungarian paprika

2   teaspoons ground cumin

1   egg, lightly beaten

Salt and freshly ground pepper to taste

6   sheets phyllo dough, thawed

1   egg, lightly beaten

Vegetable oil for frying

Lemon wedges for garnish

To make the filling: In a large skillet, cook the beef and the lamb over medium-high heat, breaking up lumps with a fork, for 2 to 3 minutes. Add the onion and garlic, and cook, stirring, until the mixture is almost dry, 10 to 12 minutes. Remove from the heat and let cool. In a medium bowl, combine the meat with the mint, parsley, paprika, cumin, egg, salt, and pepper. Set aside.

To make triangular-shaped briouats: Stack the phyllo sheets on a work surface. With the long edge of the phyllo toward you, and using a sharp knife, cut through the stacked sheets of dough to make 4 equal sections, each about 4½ inches wide. Work with 1 strip of phyllo at a time, keeping the rest of the phyllo covered with a damp towel so it will not become brittle. Place 1 tablespoon of the filling about 1 inch from the bottom edge of the strip. Fold a corner of the strip over the filling so the bottom edge is flush with the long edge. Continue folding, as you would a flag, to obtain a triangular shape. Use the beaten egg to seal the free edge. Repeat the process until all the filling has been used.

To make egg roll–shaped briouats: With the long edge of the phyllo facing you, and using a sharp knife, cut vertically through the stacked sheets of dough to make 4 equal sections, each about 4½ inches wide. Work with 1 strip of phyllo at a time, keeping the rest of the phyllo covered with a damp towel. Place 1 tablespoon of the filling at the base of the strip. Fold over the long sides and roll up. Use the beaten egg to seal the free edge. Repeat the process until all the filling is used.

The briouats are now ready for frying or freezing (see Note). To fry, preheat the oven to 200 degrees F. In a heavy, medium saucepan, heat 2 inches of oil to 325 degrees F, or until a piece of phyllo dropped into it sizzles instantly. Fry a few of the briouats until golden, about 6 to 8 minutes. Using a slotted spoon, transfer to paper towels to drain. Keep warm in the oven while frying the remaining briouats in small batches. Serve immediately, with lemon wedges.

Note: To freeze uncooked briouats, place them on a baking sheet in a single layer without touching. Freeze them, then transfer to an airtight container, separating them with waxed paper or plastic wrap. Store in the freezer for up to 2 months. Do not thaw the pastries before frying.

BRIOUAT B'KEMROON

Briouats of Shrimp and Chinese Rice Vermicelli

As a French protectorate from 1912 until 1956, Morocco became home to a number of French-speaking immigrants, including some from the former French colony of Indochina. Through their influence, Chinese rice vermicelli have become a common item in almost every large city *marché*, or market. Rice vermicelli have predictably found their way into a number of Moroccan recipes, including this one for briouats. My friend Ahlam Lemseffer even serves them Vietnamese style, wrapped in fresh lettuce and cilantro!

Makes about 2 dozen briouats

Filling:

2 ounces Chinese rice vermicelli

2 tablespoons olive oil

1 onion, finely chopped

12 ounces medium shrimp, peeled and deveined

1 teaspoon sweet Hungarian paprika

3 tablespoons minced fresh cilantro

½ teaspoon ground cumin

2 teaspoons lemon juice

3 tablespoons minced fresh flat-leaf parsley

2 teaspoons salt

Freshly ground pepper to taste

6 sheets phyllo dough, thawed

1 egg, lightly beaten

Vegetable oil for frying

To make the filling: In a medium bowl, cover the vermicelli with hot water. Let stand for 10 to 12 minutes. Transfer to a colander and drain well. Finely chop the vermicelli, return them to the bowl, and set aside.

In the meantime, in a large skillet over medium-high heat, heat the oil. Cook the onion and shrimp, stirring occasionally, until the shrimp turns pink, about 3 to 4 minutes. Remove from heat and let cool. Coarsely chop the shrimp. Combine the shrimp and onion mixture with the vermicelli, paprika, cilantro, cumin, lemon juice, parsley, salt, and pepper. Set aside.

To make triangular-shaped briouats: Set the stacked phyllo on a work surface. With the long edge of the phyllo toward you, and using a sharp knife, cut through the stacked sheets of

(continued)

dough to make 4 equal sections, each about 4 1/2 inches wide. Work with 1 strip of phyllo at a time, keeping the rest of the phyllo covered with a damp towel. Place 1 tablespoon of the filling about 1 inch from the bottom edge of the strip. Fold a corner of the strip over the filling so the bottom edge is flush with the long edge. Continue folding, as you would a flag, to obtain a triangular shape. Use the beaten egg to seal the free edge. Repeat the process until all the filling has been used.

To make egg roll–shaped briouats: With the long edge of the phyllo facing you, and using a sharp knife, cut vertically through the stacked sheets of dough to make 4 equal sections, each about 4 1/2 inches wide. Work with 1 strip of phyllo at a time, keeping the rest of the phyllo covered with a damp towel. Place 1 tablespoon of the filling at the base of the strip. Fold over the long sides and roll up. Use the beaten egg to seal the free edge. Repeat the process until all the filling is used.

The briouats are now ready for frying or freezing (see Note, page 77). To fry, preheat the oven to 200 degrees F. In a heavy medium saucepan, heat 2 inches of oil to 325 degrees F, or until a piece of phyllo dropped into it sizzles instantly. Fry a few of the briouats until golden, about 6 to 8 minutes. Using a slotted spoon, transfer to paper towels to drain. Keep warm in the oven while frying the remaining briouats in small batches. Serve immediately.

HOBZ BELBOULA
Barley Bread with Cumin

The art of bread making still flourishes in Moroccan households. Like young girls throughout the country, our neighbor's youngest daughter, Amal, quietly observes her mother, Aïcha, as she blends flour, salt, yeast, and water in a large earthenware platter called a *ga'saa*. After her mother kneads and shapes the dough into plump, round loaves, Amal's job is to transport them to the neighborhood *ferrane*, or public oven. First, she must imprint them with an identifying family symbol. A moment later, she disappears into the medina (old city), her bread board with its precious cargo carefully balanced on her head. This cumin-scented barley bread is one of Aïcha's specialties.

Makes two 8-inch round loaves

1 package active dry yeast
½ teaspoon sugar
1¾ cups warm (105 to 115 degrees F) water
1½ cups barley grits (see Note)
2½ cups bread flour

1½ teaspoons salt
2 teaspoons cumin seed, toasted (see page 33) and coarsely ground (see Note)
Vegetable oil for coating

In a small bowl, mix the yeast and sugar with ¼ cup of the water. Stir gently. Set aside until foamy, about 10 minutes. Reserve ¼ cup of the barley grits. In a large, shallow bowl, combine the remaining grits, the flour, salt, and cumin. Make a well in the center. Add the yeast mixture and ½ cup of the water. Blend with your hands while slowly adding the remaining water to make a soft dough. When it pulls away from the sides of the bowl, transfer it to a lightly floured board and knead until smooth and slightly tacky to the touch, 10 to 12 minutes. Shape the dough into a ball and let it rest for 2 to 3 minutes. Knead again vigorously for 1 minute.

Divide the dough into 2 equal parts. Shape each part into a ball and coat with a little oil. Lightly sprinkle 2 baking sheets with the remaining barley grits. Set a ball of dough on each baking sheet and gently flatten to 6 inches in diameter. Cover with a clean cloth. Let rise in a warm (about 75 degrees F) place, away from drafts, until doubled in size, 1 to 1½ hours.

Preheat the oven to 450 degrees F. Prick each dough disk with a toothpick in 3 or 4 places. Bake on the center rack of the oven until crusty and golden brown, 20 to 25 minutes.

Note: Boxes of barley grits are available in the cereal section of natural foods stores. To coarsely grind cumin seeds, use a spice grinder, or place the seeds in a plastic bag and crush them with a rolling pin.

HBEEZET BEL CARWIYA
Whole-Wheat Rolls with Caraway

**Makes 8
4-inch rolls**

On occasion, I like to make individual rolls rather than a large loaf of bread. I use caraway in this recipe, but you can substitute aniseed, if you prefer.

1 **package active dry yeast**
½ **teaspoon sugar**
1½ **cups warm (105 to 115 degrees F) water**
1½ **cups whole-wheat flour**
2½ **cups bread flour**

4 **tablespoons caraway seeds, toasted (see page 33) and coarsely ground (see Note)**
2 **teaspoons salt**
¼ **cup vegetable oil**
½ **cup semolina flour**

In a small bowl, mix the yeast and sugar with ¼ cup of the water. Stir gently. Set aside until foamy, about 10 minutes.

In a large, shallow bowl, combine the flours, 2 tablespoons of the caraway seeds, and salt. Make a well in the center. Add the yeast mixture and ½ cup of the water. Blend with your hands while slowly adding enough water to make a soft dough. When the dough pulls away from the sides of the bowl, transfer it to a lightly floured board and knead until smooth and slightly tacky to the touch, 10 to 12 minutes. Shape into a ball and let rest for 2 to 3 minutes. Knead again vigorously for 1 minute.

Divide the dough into 8 equal parts. Shape each one into a ball and coat with a little oil and some of the remaining seeds. Lightly sprinkle 2 baking sheets with semolina flour. Set 4 dough balls on each baking sheet and gently flatten each ball to a diameter of 3 inches. Cover with a clean cloth. Let rise in a warm (about 75 degrees F) place, away from drafts, until doubled in size, about 1 hour.

Preheat the oven to 450 degrees F. Prick each roll with a toothpick in several places. Bake one sheet at a time on the center rack of the oven until crusty and golden brown, about 20 minutes.

Note: To coarsely grind caraway seeds, use a mortar and pestle or an electric spice grinder, or place the seeds in a plastic bag and crush them with a rolling pin.

L'HAM, DJEJ.

L'HOOT, WA

L'HODRA

Meat, Poultry, Fish, and Vegetable Dishes

Tagine is perhaps the most frequently served dish in Morocco. The word *tagine* also refers to the unique glazed earthenware vessel with a distinctive conical lid in which the dish is cooked.

There are literally hundreds of variations of this exotic Moroccan stew. A popular sweet tagine combines lamb, prunes, and sesame seeds, in a sauce laced with cinnamon and ginger (page 87). Savory Djej M'kalli (page 91), one of Morocco's most renowned tagines, acquires its tart, sumptuous flavor from a blend of saffron, turmeric, and preserved lemons, a condiment unique to North African cuisine. Preserved lemons are often combined with seafood tagines redolent with chermoula, a classic marinade blending cumin, paprika, garlic, cilantro, and lemon juice. Exotically spiced meatballs simmered in sweet onion-raisin sauce (page 93) also belong to Morocco's extensive repertoire of tagines. Tagines are traditionally served with plenty of warm, crusty bread used to scoop up tender pieces of meat and vegetables, or to sop up the unctuous sauce from the communal dish.

Grilled and roasted meats also play a prominent role in Morocco's cuisine. No tribal feast, or *moussem,* would be complete without the presentation of the succulent whole roasted lamb called *mechoui.* Equally delicious are the spicy chunks of charcoal-grilled lamb or beef and the juicy patties of herb-scented ground meat called *kefta* sold in tiny open-air restaurants and by street vendors in every Moroccan souk (market) and medina (old city).

With the exception of Preserved Lemons (page 36) and Smen (page 38), both of which you can easily make at home, the ingredients for the following recipes are readily found in most American supermarkets.

TAGINE BIL KOK

Tagine of Lamb with Prunes

The Centre de Formation en Restauration Traditionnelle, a government-sponsored cooking school in Rabat, is dedicated to preserving the art of traditional Moroccan gastronomy. The students, all young women, will go on to staff Morocco's embassies and consulates around the world. This classic tagine recipe, given to me by the Centre's former director, Monsieur Tamer, is part of the school's delectable curriculum.

Serves 4

2 tablespoons olive oil

1 teaspoon ground turmeric

1 teaspoon ground ginger

2 pounds leg of lamb, trimmed of fat and cut into 2-inch chunks

2 onions

1 cup chicken broth

8 threads Spanish saffron, toasted and crushed (see page 32)

15 fresh cilantro sprigs, tied with cotton string

1 cup pitted prunes

2 tablespoons honey

1 teaspoon ground cinnamon

½ teaspoon pepper

Salt to taste

1 tablespoon unhulled sesame seeds, toasted (see page 33)

Hobz Belboula (page 81) or other crusty bread for serving

In a small Dutch oven or enameled casserole over medium-high heat, heat the olive oil and sauté the turmeric, ginger, and lamb until the meat is well coated and lightly browned, 2 to 3 minutes. Finely dice one of the onions. Add it to the meat along with the broth, saffron, and cilantro. Cover and reduce the heat to medium-low. Cook until the meat is fork tender, 1 to 1½ hours. Discard the cilantro.

Preheat the oven to 200 degrees F. With a slotted spoon, transfer the meat to an ovenproof dish and keep warm in the oven until ready to serve. Bring the sauce in the casserole back to a simmer.

Finely slice the remaining onion. Add it, along with the prunes, honey, cinnamon, and pepper to the simmering sauce. Season with salt. Cook until the mixture thickens somewhat, 6 to 8 minutes. Spoon the prune sauce over the meat and sprinkle the dish with the sesame seeds. Serve with warm bread.

TAGINE B'GA'RAA SGHIRA WA MATISHA MIEB'SA

Tagine of Lamb, Zucchini, Potatoes, and Sun-Dried Tomatoes

This tagine makes delicious use of the summer vegetables available in country souks and city markets. I have added my own twist to this recipe by using sun-dried tomatoes, a condiment found mainly in northern Morocco. You can purchase sun-dried tomatoes in most supermarkets in the United States. To dry your own, see page 43.

Serves 4

3   tablespoons olive oil

2   onions, finely diced

1½ pounds lamb shoulder, cut into 3-inch chunks

1   teaspoon ground turmeric

10 threads Spanish saffron, toasted and crushed (see page 32)

10 fresh cilantro sprigs, tied with cotton string

20 fresh flat-leaf parsley sprigs, tied with cotton string

2   cups chicken broth

1   pound baby carrots, scrubbed

¼   cup sun-dried tomatoes, plumped and cut into ¼-inch-thick strips

3   zucchini

3   potatoes, peeled and quartered

Salt and freshly ground pepper to taste

Preheat the oven to 350 degrees F. In a medium Dutch oven over medium-high heat, heat 2 tablespoons of the olive oil and cook the onions, stirring occasionally, until tender, 4 to 5 minutes. Add the meat, turmeric, and saffron. Sauté until the meat is coated with the spices, 2 to 3 minutes. Add the cilantro, parsley, broth, carrots, and half of the sun-dried tomatoes. Cover and bake until the meat is tender, 1½ to 2 hours. Discard the cilantro and parsley. With a slotted spoon, transfer the meat and carrots to a medium saucepan and keep warm.

Peel and slice 2 of the zucchini and add them to the sauce in the casserole, along with the potatoes. Cover and return the casserole to the oven. Bake until the potatoes are tender, 30 to 35 minutes. Remove from the oven and lightly mash the cooked zucchini into the sauce. Set aside.

Meanwhile, cut the remaining zucchini into sticks. In a small skillet over medium heat, heat the remaining 1 tablespoon olive oil and sauté the zucchini and the remaining sun-dried tomatoes until the zucchini turns golden, 4 to 5 minutes. Set aside.

Reheat the meat and carrots. Heap them on a large platter and arrange the potatoes and the zucchini mixture around the meat. Pour the remaining sauce over the dish and serve.

TREDA

Tagine of Chicken and Lentils with Fenugreek

Treda is a delicious and inexpensive stew that is served over pieces of crusty bread. It epitomizes Moroccan home-style cooking. Because it is not considered an elegant recipe, it is rarely served outside the home. I learned how to make this dish from our sixteen-year-old neighbor, Rachida Rahmoun, who took over the duties in the family kitchen following the death of her mother several years ago. I enjoyed watching her as she intuitively measured the amounts of herbs and spices the way her mother had taught her, following the Moroccan adage, *"Eenek mi zaanek"* ("Your eyes are your scale"). *Halba,* or fenugreek, gives this dish a unique, slightly bitter flavor. You can use day-old Hobz Belboula (page 81) or other crusty bread.

Serves 6

2 tablespoons olive oil	6 cups water
2 onions, sliced	30 fresh cilantro sprigs, tied with cotton string
1 large tomato, peeled and seeded (see page 33)	¼ cup fenugreek seeds
1 three-pound chicken cut into serving pieces, or 2½ pounds chicken thighs	¾ cup dried lentils, rinsed and drained
2 teaspoons pepper	6 cups 1-inch cubes day-old bread (about 1 pound)
1 teaspoon ground turmeric	Freshly ground pepper to taste
1½ teaspoons salt	Fresh cilantro leaves for garnish

In a medium Dutch oven or enameled casserole over high heat, heat the oil and sauté the onions, tomato, chicken, pepper, turmeric, and salt until the onions are tender, 5 to 8 minutes. Add the water, cilantro, and fenugreek seeds. Reduce heat to medium. Cover and cook until the chicken is tender, 40 to 45 minutes. Add the lentils and continue cooking until they are tender, 20 to 25 minutes. Discard the cilantro.

Spread the pieces of bread over the bottom of a wide, shallow serving platter. With a slotted spoon, remove the chicken from the pot and distribute it evenly over the bread. Spoon the lentils over the chicken. Ladle the broth over the dish so it soaks into the bread. Sprinkle with pepper. Garnish with the cilantro leaves. Serve immediately, with any remaining broth on the side.

DJEJ M'KALLI B'L'HAMD MARKAD
Tagine of Chicken with Preserved Lemons and Artichoke Hearts

Serves 4 to 6

You must use Preserved Lemons (see page 36) to get the authentic flavor of this unusual tagine. Moroccan cooks prefer small fresh artichokes that have been boiled and trimmed of their leaves and fuzzy choke. In season, I like to use fresh baby artichokes. If you substitute canned artichoke hearts, drain and blanch them in boiling water for 1 minute. Drain before proceeding with the recipe.

2 tablespoons butter

2 tablespoons olive oil

2 teaspoons sweet Hungarian paprika

½ teaspoon ground ginger

½ teaspoon pepper

3 pounds chicken, cut up

1 onion, finely diced

1 cup chicken broth

8 threads Spanish saffron, toasted and crushed (see page 32)

10 sprigs fresh cilantro, tied with cotton string

20 sprigs fresh flat-leaf parsley, tied with cotton string

1 tablespoon fresh lemon juice

1 tablespoon Preserved Lemon pulp (page 36)

12 baby artichokes, trimmed of any tough outer leaves, or 6 medium artichokes, boiled, trimmed of leaves and choke, and quartered, or one 14-ounce can artichoke hearts, drained

Rind of 2 Preserved Lemons (page 36), cut into thin strips

Fresh cilantro leaves for garnish

Hobz Belboula (page 81) or pita bread for serving

Preheat the oven to 400 degrees F. In a medium Dutch oven, melt the butter over medium-high heat. Add the olive oil, paprika, ginger, pepper, and chicken. Cook, stirring to coat, for 1 to 2 minutes. (Do not overcook, or the spices will turn bitter.) Add the onion, broth, saffron, cilantro, and parsley. Cover tightly and bake until the chicken is tender, 50 to 55 minutes.

Remove from the oven. With a slotted spoon, transfer the chicken to an ovenproof dish, leaving the sauce in the pan. Discard the parsley and cilantro. Reduce the oven temperature to 200 degrees F and return the chicken to the oven to keep warm. Bring the sauce to a simmer on top of the stove. Add the lemon juice, lemon pulp, and artichokes. Stir gently until the artichokes are heated through, 4 to 5 minutes. Gently stir the strips of lemon rind into the sauce.

Mound the reserved chicken in the center of a serving platter and surround it with the artichokes. Spoon the sauce over the dish. Garnish with cilantro leaves. Serve with warm bread.

TEMRIKA MESLALLA
Garlic Beef with Cracked Green Olives

Temrika is served on the eve of the Sabbath in Sephardic homes. My Friend Danielle Mamane of Fez makes her temrika with whole heads of garlic. Don't be intimidated, however, for garlic loses much of its pungency once it is baked. Spread the butterlike garlic pulp on a piece of fresh bread. You just might become addicted!

Serves 4

3 tablespoons olive oil

1½ pounds lean beef chuck, cut into 2-inch chunks

2 pounds tomatoes, coarsely chopped

1 tablespoon ground cumin

½ teaspoon pepper

8 ounces pitted cracked green olives (see Note)

4 whole heads of garlic, papery outer skins removed

1 tablespoon fresh lemon juice

¼ cup minced fresh flat-leaf parsley

Hobz Belboula (page 81) or other crusty bread for serving

Preheat the oven to 350 degrees F. In a medium Dutch oven or enameled casserole over medium-high heat, heat the olive oil and cook the beef, stirring until it is lightly browned, 3 to 4 minutes. Add the tomatoes, cumin, pepper, and olives. Nestle the heads of garlic among the chunks of meat. Cover and bake until the meat is tender, 50 minutes to 1 hour. Remove from the oven. With a slotted spoon, transfer the meat and the garlic to a serving platter and keep warm.

Reheat the pan juices over medium heat and stir in the lemon juice. Cook, stirring, until the sauce is reduced by a third. Pour it over the reserved meat. Sprinkle with the parsley and serve immediately with warm bread.

Note: To order Moroccan olives, see Mail-Order Sources, page 150. Black olives are not generally used for this tagine.

KEFTA MAHCHIYA

Stuffed Meatballs with Dried Fruit in Sweet Onion Sauce

There aren't enough hours in the day for Naïma Bounaïm, a busy elementary school principal from Casablanca, whose grandfather sold Dar Zitoun to my father. Yet, she took time out of her hectic schedule to prepare this delightful dish for me. Sometimes, as the spirit moves her, Naïma adds dates, dried apricots, or figs to her sauce, instead of raisins. *"Cette recette, c'est la recette de la créativité"* ("This recipe is the recipe of creativity"), says my friend with an infectious laugh. The meatballs are also delicious when cooked in a tomato sauce like the one for Yapraa on page 96.

Serves 6

Sauce:

2 tablespoons vegetable oil

5 onions (about 2 pounds), thinly sliced

1 tomato, peeled, seeded and coarsely chopped (see page 33)

1 teaspoon Ras el Hanout spice blend (page 41)

1 teaspoon ground cinnamon

1 teaspoon ground ginger

10 saffron threads, toasted and crushed (see page 32)

5 whole cloves

1 cup water

Salt and freshly ground pepper to taste

1 cup seedless raisins, plumped in warm water and drained, or 1 cup mixed chopped dried fruits

1 tablespoon honey

Kefta:

1 pound twice-ground sirloin

1 small onion, grated

½ cup dried bread crumbs

3 eggs

1 teaspoon Ras el Hanout spice blend (page 41)

2 teaspoons salt

Freshly ground pepper to taste

2 cups water

1 cup long-grain white rice

Ground cinnamon for garnish

½ cup whole blanched almonds, toasted (see page 33)

To make the sauce: In a medium Dutch oven or enameled casserole over medium-high heat, heat the oil and add the onions, tomato, ras el hanout, cinnamon, ginger, saffron, cloves,

(continued)

and water. Cook, stirring occasionally, until the sauce thickens somewhat, 10 to 15 minutes. Discard the cloves. Season with salt and pepper. Add the raisins or dried fruit and honey. Lower the heat to a simmer.

To make the kefta: Mix the ground sirloin and grated onion. In a large bowl, combine the meat, bread crumbs, 1 lightly beaten egg, ras el hanout, 1 teaspoon of the salt, and pepper. Mix well, using your hands. Let stand 10 minutes.

To cook the rice: In a medium saucepan, bring the water and the remaining 1 teaspoon salt to a boil. Add the rice in a slow stream and cover. Reduce heat to medium. Cook until the water is absorbed and the rice is tender, 15 to 18 minutes. Remove from heat and set aside, covered.

In a small saucepan of slowly boiling water, cook the 2 remaining eggs for 8 to 10 minutes. Drain and place in a bowl of cold water to cool for 10 to 20 minutes. Shell the eggs and cut each one into 6 wedges. Set aside.

To assemble the kefta: Using the fingers of one hand, flatten 2 tablespoons of ground meat in the palm of the opposite hand to form a thin patty about 3 inches in diameter. Place a wedge of egg in the center. Fold the meat around the egg and seal the edges. Set aside on a platter. Continue until all the meat is used.

Set the egg-filled kefta in the simmering onion sauce. Do not stir. Cover and simmer until the meat is cooked through, 10 to 12 minutes.

Fill a small bowl with the cooked rice and invert it in a mound in the center of a large circular platter. Decorate the rice with cinnamon, creating stripes that run from the center to the base like the spokes of a wheel. Garnish the rice with toasted almonds. Arrange the kefta around the base of the rice and cover them with the onion sauce. Serve immediately.

YAPRAA
Beef and Turkey Croquettes

Makes 20 to 22 croquettes

Danielle Mamane, a lifelong resident of Fez, has an extensive repertoire of family Sephardic recipes. She serves these unusually spiced, savory croquettes on the eve of the Jewish Sabbath. Sometimes, Danielle prepares smaller croquettes as hors d'oeuvres.

4 onions, chopped

3 garlic cloves

12 fresh flat-leaf parsley sprigs

6 fresh cilantro sprigs

4 eggs

1 pound twice-ground sirloin

1 pound twice-ground turkey

2 pieces baguette (about 4 inches each), soaked in ½ cup water

½ teaspoon ground ginger

¼ teaspoon ground cloves

1½ teaspoons ground mace

¼ teaspoon freshly grated nutmeg

1 teaspoon pepper, plus pepper to taste

2 teaspoons salt, plus salt to taste

2 pounds tomatoes, peeled, seeded, and coarsely chopped (see page 33)

2 tablespoons capers, drained

Oil for deep-frying

1 cup superfine durum-wheat semolina flour

In a blender or food processor, grind 2 of the onions with the garlic, parsley, cilantro, and 2 of the eggs. In a large bowl, combine the onion mixture, sirloin, turkey, soaked bread, ginger, cloves, mace, nutmeg, the 1 teaspoon pepper, and the 2 teaspoons salt. Mix well with your hands. Refrigerate.

Meanwhile, finely chop the 2 remaining onions. In a large enameled saucepan, combine the onions and tomatoes. Cook over medium heat until the sauce thickens somewhat, 20 to 25 minutes. Stir in the capers and season with salt and pepper to taste. Keep warm.

Wet your hands. Shape ¼-cup portions of the meat mixture into 4-inch long croquettes.

Preheat the oven to 200 degrees F. In a large skillet, pour oil to a depth of 1½ inches and heat over medium heat until a piece of meat sizzles instantly. (If the temperature of the oil is too high, the outside of the croquettes will turn brown while the inside will remain raw.) Pour the semolina onto a shallow plate. In another bowl, beat the 2 remaining eggs.

Roll each croquette in the beaten egg, then in the semolina. Fry the croquettes without overcrowding, turning each one carefully with tongs until it becomes lightly brown, 10 to 12 minutes. Drain on paper towels. Transfer to an ovenproof dish and keep warm in the oven.

Pour some of the tomato sauce onto a large serving platter, set the croquettes in the sauce, and serve immediately with the remaining sauce on the side.

TAGINE M'DERBEL BERANIYA

Tagine of Chicken with Eggplant and Sun-Dried Tomatoes

This is my adaptation of the exotic eggplant dish named after Boran, a Persian vizier's daughter who married a powerful ninth-century caliph in a wedding that was "the medieval byword for lavishness," according to food historian Charles Perry.

Serves 6

5 tablespoons olive oil	10 fresh flat-leaf parsley sprigs, tied with cotton string
2 onions, finely chopped	2 globe eggplants, peeled and cut into 1/4-inch-thick slices
2 teaspoons ground ginger	1/4 cup Sun-Dried Tomatoes (page 43) plumped in warm water, drained, and diced
1 teaspoon ground cinnamon	
2 pounds chicken, cut into serving pieces	Salt and freshly ground pepper to taste
1 cup chicken broth	Hobz Belboula (page 81) or other crusty bread for serving
8 threads Spanish saffron, toasted and crushed (see page 32)	
10 fresh cilantro sprigs, tied with cotton string	

In a medium Dutch oven over medium-high heat, heat 3 tablespoons of the olive oil. Add the onions, ginger, and cinnamon, and sauté until the onions are translucent, 2 to 3 minutes. Add the chicken, and sauté until it turns golden, 5 to 6 minutes. Reduce the heat to medium and add the broth, saffron, cilantro, and parsley. Cover and cook until the chicken is tender and the juices run clear, 45 to 50 minutes. Meanwhile, place the eggplant slices on a clean towel. Salt them lightly on both sides. Let sit for 15 to 20 minutes. Pat dry with the towel.

Preheat the broiler. Place the eggplant slices on a baking sheet lined with aluminum foil. Lightly brush the slices with the remaining 2 tablespoons of olive oil. Broil until light brown, 5 to 6 minutes on each side. Set aside. Reduce the oven heat to 200 degrees F.

When the chicken is cooked, transfer it to a baking dish and keep warm in the oven. Discard the parsley and cilantro. Keep the sauce simmering on the stove. Reserve 10 eggplant slices for garnish. Add the remaining eggplant and the sun-dried tomatoes to the sauce and mash them lightly in the pan juices. Season with salt and pepper. Cook, stirring, until the sauce thickens somewhat, 4 to 5 minutes.

Spoon this mixture on the bottom of a large, shallow platter. Top with the chicken and garnish with the reserved eggplant slices. Serve with warm bread.

TAGINE M'HAMMAR
Stuffed Cornish Hens in Sweet Paprika Sauce

Serves 4

In this tagine, couscous-stuffed Cornish hens are simmered in a paprika-laced *m'hammar* sauce. The pungent and exotic preserved butter called *smen* gives the couscous its distinctive flavor. You may, however, prefer to substitute equal amounts of butter and olive oil for the smen.

2 cups chicken broth

12 threads Spanish saffron, toasted and crushed (see page 32)

½ cup couscous

2 tablespoons pine nuts, toasted (see page 33)

5 tablespoons minced fresh flat-leaf parsley

2 teaspoons Smen (page 38)

2 tablespoons olive oil

2 teaspoons sweet Hungarian paprika

½ teaspoon ground cumin

2 Cornish game hens, rinsed and patted dry

Salt and freshly ground pepper to taste

2 onions, finely chopped

¼ cup minced fresh cilantro

4 tablespoons butter

Hobz Belboula (page 81) or other crusty bread for serving

In a medium saucepan, bring 1 cup of the chicken broth and 4 of the saffron threads to a boil. Gradually stir in the couscous. Cover, remove from heat, and let stand for 5 minutes. Combine the couscous with 1 tablespoon of the pine nuts, half of the minced parsley, and the smen. Set aside.

In a large bowl, mix the olive oil with the remaining 8 saffron threads, the paprika, and cumin. Using your hands, coat the Cornish hens with this mixture. Salt and pepper the cavities. Spoon an equal portion of couscous inside the cavity of each hen. Place the hens snugly in a small Dutch oven or deep enameled casserole. Surround the hens with the remaining parsley, onions, cilantro, and the remaining 1 cup broth. Sprinkle with salt and pepper. Cover and cook over medium heat until the hens are tender and the juices run clear when a thigh is pierced with a fork, about 1 hour.

In a large skillet, melt the butter over medium-high heat. Transfer the hens to the skillet. Carefully turn them until they are uniformly reddish-gold. Bring the sauce in the Dutch oven or casserole to a simmer.

Place the hens in the center of a large, shallow platter. Spoon the sauce around the dish and sprinkle with the remaining pine nuts. Serve immediately with warm bread.

TAGINE B'BEID
Egg Tagine with Olives, Onions, and Cilantro

Serves 4 to 6

This is a variation of an egg tagine that I first tasted years ago at a small restaurant across the shallow Assif el Mellah stream from the historic and picturesque kasbah of Aït Ben Haddou. The view was spectacular, and so was the tagine. I love to prepare it when I am in the mood for a light supper. I also serve it inside a hollowed-out brioche as a brunch entree.

3 tomatoes, peeled, seeded, and coarsely chopped (see page 33)
20 green olives, pitted
2 tablespoons olive oil
2 onions, very finely diced
½ teaspoon sugar
2 garlic cloves, minced
1 bay leaf

8 eggs
¼ cup minced fresh cilantro
2 teaspoons ground cumin
Salt and freshly ground pepper to taste
Fresh cilantro leaves for garnish
Hobz Belboula (page 81) or other crusty bread for serving

Set the tomatoes in a colander to drain. Meanwhile, in a small saucepan of boiling water, blanch the olives for 1 minute. Drain and chop coarsely. Set aside.

In a medium skillet over medium-high heat, heat the olive oil and cook the onions, olives, and sugar, stirring occasionally, until the onions are lightly caramelized, 8 to 10 minutes. Add the tomatoes, garlic, and bay leaf. Stir to blend and mash them lightly with a fork. Reduce heat to low and simmer until most of the liquid evaporates, 15 to 20 minutes. Discard the bay leaf.

In a medium bowl, beat the eggs with the cilantro, cumin, salt, and pepper. Pour them into the simmering tomato sauce. Stir gently until the eggs are set. Transfer to a shallow serving bowl and garnish with cilantro leaves. Serve immediately with warm bread.

DJEJ M'FOOWER
Naïma's Steamed Chicken

Increasing numbers of modern Moroccan cooks, like my friend economist Naïma Lakhal, watch the fat in their diets. For this reason, Naïma prefers to steam her chicken rather than cook it in a traditional tagine. She stuffs the chicken with fresh herbs and presents it on a bed of seasonal vegetables with broth on the side. I find it a little more convenient to plate the dish before bringing it to the table. I love to use any leftover broth to make a soup like Chorba (page 49).

Serves 6

2	lemons	½	teaspoon ground cumin
1	teaspoon salt	3	teaspoons sweet Hungarian paprika
1	teaspoon ground ginger	1	teaspoon salt
1	four-pound chicken	½	teaspoon pepper
¼	cup minced fresh cilantro (reserve stems)	2	bay leaves
⅔	cup minced fresh flat-leaf parsley sprigs (reserve stems)	1	onion, studded with 4 cloves
		2	pounds small new potatoes, peeled
1	fresh bird's tongue or jalapeno chili, seeded (optional)	1	pound baby carrots, scrubbed
		1	pound green beans
3	garlic cloves, minced	1	red bell pepper, seeded, deribbed, and diced

The day before or a few hours ahead, remove the zest from the lemons with a vegetable peeler or zester. Finely dice and set aside. Juice the lemons. In a small bowl, mix the lemon juice, salt, and ginger. Rub the mixture over the chicken and spoon some into the cavity. Refrigerate the chicken.

In a medium bowl, combine the lemon zest with the cilantro, parsley, chili (if using), garlic, cumin, and 2 teaspoons of the paprika. Stir in the salt and pepper and stuff the cavity of the chicken with the mixture. Rub the remaining 1 teaspoon paprika over the outer skin of the chicken.

Fill a large soup pot, steamer, or the bottom of a couscoussière with water and bring it to a boil. Add the bay leaves, the clove-studded onion, and the reserved herb stems to the pot. Layer the bottom of a colander, large steamer basket, or top part of the couscoussière with half the potatoes, carrots, green beans, and bell pepper. Set the chicken on top and surround it with the remaining vegetables. Place the colander on top of the soup pot, or fit the steamer basket into the steamer or the top part into the couscoussière. Seal the two parts with a strip of damp cloth to prevent the steam from escaping. Cover the colander, basket, or top part of the couscoussière tightly with a lid or aluminum foil.

Steam until the chicken is tender and the juices run clear, 1 1/2 to 2 hours. Discard the vegetables in the broth. Season the broth with salt and pepper. With a spoon, remove the chicken stuffing and transfer it to a large bowl. Mix it with 4 or 5 cups of the broth. Set aside. Carve the chicken and set aside.

Line 6 shallow soup plates with the steamed vegetables. Top each serving with a piece of chicken and spoon the stuffing/broth mixture over the plate. Serve immediately, with additional broth on the side.

Strain any remaining broth into a large container. Chill and discard the fat. Freeze or refrigerate for another use.

TAGINE BIL HOOT
Tagine of Fish

Moroccan cooks take advantage of the bounty harvested from the rich fishing grounds just off the Mediterranean and Atlantic coasts. You can use any firm-fleshed fish for this dish, like mahimahi, red snapper, sea bass, or orange roughy. In Morocco, small sticks of bamboo are often crisscrossed at the bottom of the cooking vessel to prevent the fish from sticking to the pan. I use carrot slices instead.

Serves 4

¼ cup minced fresh flat-leaf parsley

2 tablespoons minced fresh cilantro

½ cup olive oil

2 teaspoons sweet Hungarian paprika

8 threads Spanish saffron, toasted and crushed (see page 32)

1 teaspoon ground ginger

1 lemon

4 six-ounce boned fish fillets

4 tomatoes, peeled, seeded, and coarsely chopped (see page 33)

2 garlic cloves, minced

1 teaspoon ground cumin

Salt and freshly ground pepper to taste

2 carrots, peeled and sliced diagonally

1 onion, thinly sliced

1 tablespoon preserved lemon pulp (page 36)

12 green or black olives, pitted

Fresh parsley or cilantro leaves for garnish

In a large bowl, mix the parsley, cilantro, olive oil, paprika, saffron, and ginger. Add the juice of half of the lemon. Coat the fish fillets with this mixture and refrigerate for 1 to 2 hours, turning over once or twice. Cut the other lemon half into very thin slices. Set aside.

Meanwhile, in a large saucepan, combine the tomatoes, garlic, and cumin. Cook over medium heat, stirring occasionally, until the sauce thickens slightly, 8 to 10 minutes. Season with salt and pepper. Set aside.

Place the carrot slices in a single layer on the bottom of a small Dutch oven or enameled casserole. Cover with the onion slices. Spoon the tomato sauce over the onion. Cover and cook over medium heat until the carrots are tender, 15 to 20 minutes. Remove from the heat and set the fish on top of the vegetables. Spread a little preserved lemon pulp over each fillet and top each one with a slice of lemon. Add the marinade. Surround the fish with the olives. Cover the pan once again and cook over medium heat until the fish is flaky, 10 to 12 minutes. Spoon some of the sauce over the fish. Garnish with parsley or cilantro leaves. Serve immediately.

AMBASSL' DEL GAR'AA HAMRA

Baked Pumpkin with Caramelized Onions, Cinnamon, and Almonds

I remember as a young girl shopping with Maman Darmon, my maternal great-grandmother, in Casablanca's bustling Marché Central. We would buy, among other things, bright orange wedges of fresh Mediterranean pumpkin that hung above the produce vendors' stalls. She used the vegetable frequently to prepare this old family favorite she called *cassolita,* a name that bespeaks its Andalusian roots. She always served the dish as an accompaniment to couscous. I do too, but also as a side dish for our Thanksgiving turkey! Substitute butternut, acorn, or Hubbard squash, if you prefer.

Serves 4

2   **pounds pumpkin, preferably sugar pumpkin**

½   **cup water**

¼   **cup vegetable oil**

3   **onions, thinly sliced**

4   **tablespoons slivered almonds, toasted (see page 33)**

½   **cup seedless raisins, plumped in warm water and drained**

¼   **cup sugar**

2   **teaspoons ground cinnamon**

Salt and freshly ground pepper to taste

Preheat the oven to 375 degrees F. Cut the pumpkin into 2-inch chunks. Place them in an ovenproof dish. Add the water and cover tightly. Bake until tender, 40 to 45 minutes. Let cool. Peel the pumpkin and set aside.

In a large skillet over medium heat, heat the oil and sauté the onions until tender, 5 to 6 minutes. Add 3 tablespoons of the almonds, the raisins, sugar, cinnamon, salt, and pepper. Cook, stirring, until the onions are caramelized, 15 to 20 minutes. Spread the onion mixture evenly over the peeled pumpkin. Return to the oven and bake until heated through, 10 to 15 minutes. Sprinkle with the remaining almonds and serve immediately.

TANGIA MRAKCHIYA
Bachelor's Stew Marrakesh

Historically, tangia was considered a poor man's dish, because it was popular among Morocco's unmarried workmen. It combined inexpensive cuts of meat with onions and liberal amounts of ras el hanout spice blend. The word *tangia* also refers to the earthenware amphora in which the dish is baked. After sealing the amphora with brown wrapping paper and string, bachelors could drop it off at the public oven in the morning before work, and pick it up, piping hot, on their way home for dinner. Nowadays, the dish has acquired a loftier reputation and is even featured in some of Morocco's most elegant restaurants.

Though not a bachelor, our friend and neighbor Abderrahmane Rahoule, a leading artist and ceramicist whose graceful sculptures adorn public buildings and squares throughout Morocco, often prepares this Marrakesh stew for the guests he invites to his weekend retreat inside the ramparts of the Azemmour medina (old city). I am using Rahoule's own blend of ras el hanout, which includes ginger, pepper, paprika, turmeric, and nutmeg.

Serves 6

2　tablespoons ground ginger

1　teaspoon pepper

1　teaspoon sweet Hungarian paprika

2　teaspoons ground turmeric

2　teaspoons freshly grated nutmeg

1　teaspoon ground cumin

4　garlic cloves, minced

2　teaspoons salt

½　cup vegetable oil

3　pounds lamb shoulder, cut into chunks and trimmed of fat

1　cup beef broth

3　pounds small yellow onions (about the size of golf balls), peeled

Fresh mint leaves for garnish (optional)

Hobz Belboula (page 81) or other crusty bread for serving

Preheat the oven to 350 degrees F. In a medium bowl, combine the ginger, pepper, paprika, turmeric, nutmeg, cumin, garlic, salt, and oil. Stir to blend. Coat each piece of lamb with this mixture. Set aside. Swirl the broth in the bowl that held the spices. Set aside.

Place the onions on the bottom of a Dutch oven or a large enameled baking dish. Cover with the meat. Add the reserved broth from the bowl. Cover the dish first with aluminum foil, then with a lid, to create a tight seal. Bake until the meat falls off the bones, 2 ½ to 3 hours. Skim off the fat.

Spoon the stew and some of the sauce into shallow soup plates. Garnish with mint leaves. Serve with plenty of warm bread.

MROUZIYA
Honey Spiced Lamb

Mrouziya is traditionally served during Aid el Kebir, the religious feast that commemorates the sacrifice of Abraham. The word itself is derived from Maurusia, the name the ancient Greeks gave to northwest Africa. The exquisitely seasoned dish, redolent with the exotic ras el hanout spice blend, is based on a centuries-old recipe.

"You can't hurry mrouziya," said my neighbor, Naïma Lakhmar, as she lit the coals in a *canoun*, or small charcoal brazier, in Dar Zitoun's atrium early one morning. The rhythmic sound from her heavy brass mortar reverberated through the house as she vigorously pounded spices to make ras el hanout. She slowly added her intoxicating blend to the heavy black pot atop the canoun that held the other ingredients. Exotic aromas drifted through the house over the next few hours, as Naïma periodically stirred the contents of the pot until the sauce had turned the color of dark caramel.

Serves 6

4   **pounds lamb shoulder, cut into large chunks**

3   **tablespoons ras el hanout spice blend (page 41)**

2 to 3 **cups water**

½   **cup vegetable oil**

2   **tablespoons smen (page 38)**

½   **cup honey**

¾   **cup raisins, plumped in warm water and drained**

1   **cup (5 ounces) whole blanched almonds, toasted (see page 33)**

Hobz Belboula (page 81) or other crusty bread for serving

Preheat the oven to 325 degrees F. With your hands, thoroughly coat the meat with ras el hanout. Set the meat in a heavy cast-iron pan or an enameled casserole with a heavy lid. Add the water, the oil, smen, and honey. Cover tightly. Bake until the meat falls off the bones, 3 to 4 hours.

With a slotted spoon, transfer the meat to an ovenproof dish and keep warm. Skim the fat from the sauce. Place the casserole over medium-high heat and add the raisins. Cook, stirring, until the sauce attains the consistency of maple syrup, 10 to 12 minutes. Return the meat to the sauce. Stir to coat and heat through.

Transfer the meat to a shallow platter and garnish with the toasted almonds. Serve with extra sauce on the side, and warm bread.

DAFINA
Sephardic Sabbath Stew

Dafina is served in Moroccan Sephardic homes on the Sabbath. The word *dafina* derives from the Arabic *dfenn* (to bury). Each family's clay pot of stew was traditionally buried in the coals of the public oven on Friday at noon, and retrieved the following day in time for the Sabbath lunch. My great-grandmother Maman Darmon was well known for her delicious dafina, fragrant with ginger, mace, and nutmeg. When her guests had feasted to their heart's content, she would offer everyone a small glass of her homemade *mahia,* a potent Sephardic digestif distilled from figs, dates, or raisins.

Serves 6

½ cup chickpeas, soaked and drained (see page 33)

3 pounds beef chuck, cut into 2-inch pieces

1 beef marrow bone

1 whole head of garlic, outer papery skin removed

6 onions

6 potatoes, peeled and quartered

2 yams, peeled and cut into 1-inch cubes

6 prunes, pitted

6 dried apricot halves

¼ cup pearl barley

3 cups beef broth

½ cup water

10 threads Spanish saffron, toasted and crushed (see page 32)

2 teaspoons ground mace

½ teaspoon freshly grated nutmeg

½ teaspoon ground cinnamon

Salt and freshly ground pepper to taste

3 eggs in shells, washed

Preheat the oven to 325 degrees F. In a large cast-iron pan or enameled casserole, combine the chickpeas, beef, beef bone, garlic, onions, potatoes, yams, prunes, apricots, barley, and broth. In a small bowl, mix the water with the saffron, mace, nutmeg, cinnamon, salt, and pepper. Pour over the meat. Place the eggs in the pan.

Cover with a lid or aluminum foil and bake until the meat is tender, 2 ½ to 3 hours. Increase the oven heat to 400 degrees F. Remove the lid and bake until the top of the stew turns a rich caramel color, 25 to 30 minutes. Transfer the eggs to a bowl to cool. Shell the eggs and cut them in half. The whites will have a mottled brown appearance (see Note).

Mound the meat in the center of a large platter. Spoon the remaining stew around the meat. Garnish with the egg halves and serve.

Note: To keep the egg whites white, cook the eggs separately, placing them in a small pan of slowly boiling water for 10 to 12 minutes. With a slotted spoon, transfer them to a bowl filled with cold water. Let cool for 10 to 15 minutes. Remove the shells and cut the eggs in half.

MECHOUI

Leg of Lamb with Preserved Lemon, Olive Oil, Garlic, and Cumin Marinade

Traditionally, *mechoui* refers to a whole lamb that has been spit-roasted over coals or baked inside a clay or brick oven. It is usually part of a multi-course banquet that concludes a *moussem,* or tribal festival. This recipe uses a leg of the lamb liberally coated with a mixture of preserved lemon, garlic, olive oil, and cumin. I always serve mechoui the Moroccan way, with little saucers of cumin and salt around the table for dipping. The lamb in a mechoui should always be well done.

Serves 8

1   four-pound leg of lamb, trimmed of fat
2   garlic cloves, sliced into thin slivers
¼   cup preserved lemon pulp (page 36)
2   tablespoons extra-virgin olive oil
1   teaspoon ground cumin
8   celery stalks, cut into 2-inch pieces
Freshly ground pepper to taste
Fresh mint leaves, cumin, and salt for serving

Preheat the oven to 500 degrees F. With the point of a sharp knife, make thin slits around the leg of lamb. Insert the garlic slivers. Set aside.

In a medium bowl, blend the lemon pulp, olive oil, and cumin. With your fingers, spread the paste over the leg of lamb. Completely cover the bottom of a large baking dish with the celery. Set the lamb on top. Sprinkle with pepper.

Insert a meat thermometer into the leg of lamb, taking care it doesn't come into contact with bone or fat. Bake on the center rack until a crust forms, 12 to 15 minutes. Reduce the heat to 350 degrees F. Continue baking until the thermometer registers 165 degrees to 175 degrees F, 1 ½ to 1 ¾ hours.

Remove the lamb from the oven and let stand for 10 to 15 minutes before slicing. To serve, place the lamb slices on a bed of mint leaves. Surround with the braised celery. Serve the pan juices in a separate bowl. Place saucers filled with cumin and salt around the table for dipping.

AL KOTBAN MRAKCHIYA
Shish Kabobs Marrakesh Style

Shish kabobs, also called by their French name, *brochettes*, are one of Morocco's most popular fast foods. They are cooked and served al fresco throughout the country, from small-town souks to famed Djemaa el Fna Square in the heart of Marrakesh. At dusk, this legendary and exotic gathering place takes on the surrealistic appearance of a Fellini film set. Tight circles of onlookers gather around snake charmers, fire eaters, acrobats, and fortune-tellers, while the syncopated beat of *derbouka* drums rises above the din of the crowd. The smoky aroma of freshly grilled meat drifts across the square. Vendors do a brisk business, selling spicy beef and lamb brochettes that they slide into pockets of warm bread. A pinch of cumin, some Moroccan salsa, a spoonful of harissa, and *voilà!* My mouth waters just thinking about it! You can use the same marinade for chicken, beef, or seafood.

Serves 6

1	three-pound leg of lamb
¼	cup olive oil
2	tablespoons minced fresh cilantro
2	tablespoons minced fresh flat-leaf parsley
½	onion, grated
1	tablespoon sweet Hungarian paprika
2	garlic cloves, minced
1	teaspoon ground cumin
¼	cup fresh lemon juice

1	teaspoon pepper
	Fresh mint leaves or lettuce leaves for garnish
	Fresh Tomato Salsa (recipe follows) for serving
	Hobz Belboula (page 81) or warm pita bread for serving
	Ground cumin for serving
	Salt for serving
	Harissa (page 39) for serving

Trim the lamb of fat and cut the meat into ¾-inch cubes. In a large bowl, combine the meat, olive oil, cilantro, parsley, onion, paprika, garlic, cumin, lemon juice, and pepper. Cover and refrigerate for at least 2 hours or overnight.

Prepare a fire in a charcoal grill or preheat the broiler. Thread 8 to 10 pieces of meat on metal skewers. Grill over a medium fire, turning occasionally, for about 6 to 8 minutes for medium rare. To serve, line a large platter with mint or lettuce leaves and top with the skewers. Serve with tomato salsa, plenty of warm bread, and little saucers filled with cumin, salt, and harissa on the side for dipping.

(continued)

CHLADA MATISHA WA NAHNA
Fresh Tomato Salsa

In Djemaa el Fna Square, this refreshing salsa usually accompanies brochettes.

Makes ¾ cup

2	ripe tomatoes, peeled, seeded, and coarsely chopped (see page 33)
2	green onions, tops included, finely chopped
4	fresh mint leaves, minced
¼	teaspoon sugar

Salt and freshly ground pepper to taste

In a small bowl, combine all the ingredients.

Couscous

Couscous is to Moroccans what pasta is to Italians and rice to the Chinese. The word itself refers to the granular durum wheat semolina product, as well as to the prepared dish in which it is the principal ingredient. A steaming platter of couscous is the pièce de résistance of a Moroccan dinner.

The origin of couscous (*k'seksoo* in Arabic) is uncertain. Professor Naïma Lakhal, an expert on couscous and its importance in the Moroccan economy, believes North Africa's indigenous Berbers first devised the method for its production. Other scholars give credit to the medieval Moors of Al Andalus (occupied Spain), where cookbook author Ibn Razin Al-Tudjibi-Al-Andalusi describes its use in the thirteenth century.

Each granule of couscous represents a good deed.

—Moroccan Saying

Whatever its beginnings, couscous today is of fundamental value to Moroccan culture, for dietary as well as religious and symbolic reasons. Moroccans believe it is a food that brings God's blessing upon those who consume it. For this reason, its preparation is de rigueur on holy days, especially Friday, the Moslem day of rest. Pilgrims returning from the hajj to Mecca are feted with couscous, garnished with hard boiled-eggs, as a symbol of their renewal. On the Feast of Achoura, commemorating the death of the Prophet's grandson, superstitious wives conceal morsels of *qaddid* (preserved lamb's tail) within a mound of couscous, as a means of ensuring their husband's fidelity. Many Moroccan women still prepare their own couscous granules by hand. They purchase sacks of wheat which the neighborhood miller

will grind into semolina. To make couscous, they place several handfuls of this into large, shallow, earthenware implements called *ga'saa.* While slowly adding small amounts of flour and salted water, and using their hands in a graceful, circular motion, they "roll" the mixture to form tiny granules, which they set in the sun to dry before storing.

To prepare a dish of couscous in the traditional manner, dried couscous granules are once again placed in the ga'saa, and sprinkled liberally with water. The mixture is then transferred to a metal *keskess* (colander), set snugly atop a *q'draa* (large pot) containing either water or a stew of vegetables, and meat or fish. (The two implements together are known in French as a *couscoussière.*) After sealing the seam between the keskess and q'draa with a strip of cloth dipped in a mixture of water and flour, the couscous is steamed, uncovered, until puffs of vapor emanate from the granules. The warm couscous is returned to the ga'saa, and again mixed with some water. It is transferred back to the colander, and steamed a second time until the granules become soft and plump. Finally, the tender couscous is flavored with judicious quantities of butter, olive oil, or *smen* (preserved butter, page 38) and moistened with broth from the stew. It is mounded on a large serving platter, and its "face" is artfully decorated with vegetables, meat, or fish from the q'draa.

Couscous is traditionally served in a communal dish. Moroccan diners, using the thumb and first two fingers of the right hand, incorporate small bits of meat or vegetable with the warm granules to form little balls which they deftly pop into their mouths with a flick of the thumb. Uninitiated guests, however, usually prefer to attack the steaming mountain of couscous with a soup spoon.

K'SEKSOO BEÏDAOUI
Couscous Casablanca Style

In Casablanca, Morocco's largest city and the country's commercial capital, families come together on Fridays to feast on this regional specialty, which, according to tradition, must include at least seven different kinds of seasonal vegetables as well as chicken and lamb or beef. Farmers grow many of the vegetables used in the dish in the fields of the fertile Chaouia plain on the outskirts of Dar-el-Beïda, as Casablanca is called in Arabic.

Serves 6 to 8

2 tablespoons olive oil

4 onions, thinly sliced

1 pound beef chuck or lamb shoulder, cut into 2-inch chunks

1 three-pound chicken, cut up

1 sixteen-ounce can whole tomatoes

30 fresh flat-leaf parsley sprigs, tied with cotton string

15 fresh cilantro sprigs, tied with cotton string

8 cups water

14 threads Spanish saffron, toasted and crushed (see page 32)

1 teaspoon ground turmeric

2 teaspoons ground ginger

4 carrots, peeled and cut into short sticks

4 turnips, peeled and quartered

½ cup dried chickpeas, soaked and drained (see page 33)

4 celery stalks, cut into 3-inch pieces

1 pound pumpkin, peeled and cut into 2-inch chunks

4 zucchini, quartered lengthwise

Salt and freshly ground pepper to taste

2 cups chicken broth

2 tablespoons butter

2 cups instant couscous

2 teaspoons Smen (page 38), optional

¼ cup raisins, plumped in warm water and drained

2 tablespoons Harissa (page 39), optional

In a large soup pot over medium-high heat, heat the oil and sauté the onions until tender, 4 to 5 minutes. Add the beef or lamb and chicken, and cook, stirring occasionally, until browned, 5 to 6 minutes. Add the tomatoes, parsley, cilantro, and water. Bring to a rolling boil. Cover and cook for 6 to 8 minutes. Reduce the heat to medium. Add 10 of the saffron threads, the turmeric, ginger, carrots, turnips, chickpeas, and celery. Cover and cook until the chicken is tender, 40 to 45 minutes.

Preheat the oven to 200 degrees F. With a slotted spoon, transfer the carrots, turnips, and chicken to an ovenproof dish. Cover and place in the oven to keep warm.

(continued)

Add the pumpkin and zucchini to the soup broth. Season with salt and pepper. Cover and cook until the pumpkin is tender, 15 to 20 minutes. With a slotted spoon, add the pumpkin and zucchini to the vegetables in the oven. Discard the parsley and cilantro. Keep the soup broth simmering until ready to serve.

In a medium saucepan, bring the chicken broth, butter, and remaining saffron threads to a boil. Gradually stir in the couscous and remove from heat. Cover and let stand for 5 minutes. Transfer the couscous to a large bowl. Add $\frac{1}{4}$ cup of the soup broth and the smen, if using. Fluff with a fork.

Mound the couscous on a large serving platter. Top with the cooked vegetables and surround with the meat. Garnish with raisins. In a small bowl, mix 1 cup of the soup broth with the harissa, if using. Serve on the side, along with another bowl filled with the remaining soup broth.

Note: To prepare 3 cups of instant couscous in the traditional manner, bring water or broth to a rolling boil in the bottom part of a couscoussière, or a large pot topped with a tight-fitting colander. In a large bowl, mix 1 cup of uncooked instant couscous with $\frac{3}{4}$ cup of water. Let stand until the liquid is absorbed, 5 to 10 minutes. Break up the granules with your hands and transfer them to the colander. Cook, uncovered, until you see the steam escaping through the granules, 10 to 12 minutes. Transfer the steamed couscous to a large bowl. With a fork, incorporate $\frac{1}{4}$ cup water or broth, breaking up any lumps in the process. Return the couscous to the colander and steam again for 5 to 6 minutes. Again, transfer the couscous to the bowl, and mix with 1 tablespoon olive oil, butter, or smen (page 38). Mound on a platter and garnish. Serve with additional broth on the side.

K'SEKSOO BELBOULA
Barley Couscous with Lamb and Turnips

Couscous belboula is a favorite of Morocco's Berbers, many of whom live in the barley-producing region in the southern part of the country. I love to prepare it with small young turnips that I find in early spring at my local farmers' market. They acquire a surprisingly mild flavor in this saffron-scented broth. You can make the broth with beef or chicken instead of lamb, if you prefer. Look for instant barley grits in natural foods stores.

Serves 8

2 tablespoons olive oil

2 onions, quartered

2 pounds lamb riblets or lamb shoulder, cut into chunks

8 tomatoes (about 2 pounds), peeled and coarsely chopped (see page 33)

8 cups water

20 fresh cilantro sprigs, tied with cotton string

10 fresh flat-leaf parsley sprigs, tied with cotton string

8 small turnips, halved

10 small carrots, peeled

2 teaspoons ground turmeric

10 threads Spanish saffron, toasted and crushed (see page 32)

1 teaspoon pepper

2 red bell peppers

2½ teaspoons salt

2 cups chicken broth

2 tablespoons butter

2 cups instant barley grits

2 teaspoons Smen (page 38)

In a Dutch oven or a large soup pot over medium-high heat, heat the oil and sauté the onions until tender, 5 to 6 minutes. Add the lamb and cook until browned, 4 to 5 minutes. Add the tomatoes, water, cilantro, parsley, turnips, carrots, turmeric, and saffron. Reduce the heat to medium. Cover, and cook until the meat is tender, 40 to 45 minutes. Season with pepper.

Preheat the oven to 200 degrees F. With a slotted spoon, transfer the vegetables to an oven-proof dish. Cover and keep warm. Keep the soup broth and the meat simmering in the pot. Add the bell peppers and cook until tender, 5 to 6 minutes. Discard the cilantro and parsley. Season with salt.

In a large saucepan, bring the chicken broth and butter to a boil over medium-high heat. Gradually stir in the barley grits and remove from the heat. Cover and let stand for 5 minutes. Transfer the grits to a large bowl. Add ¼ cup of the soup broth and fluff with a fork to break up any lumps. Stir in the smen.

Arrange the cooked barley grits around the perimeter of a large serving platter. Place the vegetables and the meat in the center. Serve with the remaining soup broth on the side.

K'SEKSOO BIL HOOT OUALIDI

Fish Couscous Oualidia

Oualidia is a picturesque lagoon on Morocco's Atlantic Coast renowned for its seafood, which local chef Brahim Mahdi features on his menu at the landmark L'Hippocampe restaurant. Every Friday evening, he prepares this delightful fish couscous for his patrons. Use a mild, firm-fleshed fish like sea bass, orange roughy, or red snapper.

Serves 8

2 cups water	6 tomatoes (about 1½ pounds), quartered
2 tablespoons butter	4 carrots, peeled and cut into 3-inch sticks
2 cups instant couscous	2 turnips, peeled and cut into wedges
4 tablespoons olive oil	6 zucchini, cut into 3-inch sticks
1 tablespoon sweet Hungarian paprika	2 red bell peppers, seeded, deribbed, and quartered lengthwise
2 teaspoons ground cumin	3 pounds boned fish fillets
2 teaspoons ground turmeric	2 garlic cloves, sliced
1 teaspoon freshly ground pepper	1 pound fresh mussels, scrubbed and debearded
8 cups water or Fish Stock (recipe follows)	1 pound medium shrimp, shelled and deveined
30 fresh flat-leaf parsley sprigs, tied with cotton string	Harissa (page 39), for serving
20 fresh cilantro sprigs, tied with cotton string	

Preheat the oven to 200 degrees F. To make the couscous, in a medium saucepan, bring the water and butter to a boil. Gradually stir in the couscous and remove from the heat. Cover and let stand 5 minutes. Transfer the couscous to an ovenproof dish. Cover and keep warm.

In a large soup pot over medium heat, heat 2 tablespoons of the olive oil and stir in the paprika, cumin, turmeric, and pepper. Cook, stirring, until the spices give off a fragrant aroma, 1 to 2 minutes. Add the water or stock, parsley, cilantro, tomatoes, carrots, and turnips. Cover and bring to a boil. Cook until the carrots are tender, 12 to 15 minutes. Add the zucchini and peppers, and cook until tender, 8 to 10 minutes. With a slotted spoon, transfer the vegetables to an ovenproof dish. Cover and keep warm. Keep the broth simmering on the stove.

Cut the fish fillets into 3-inch pieces. In a medium skillet over medium-high heat, heat the remaining 2 tablespoons olive oil and sauté the garlic until golden, 2 to 3 minutes. Discard the garlic. Cook the fish until light brown, 1 to 2 minutes on each side. Add the fish, mussels, and shrimp to the broth in the pot. Cook until the fish begins to separate into flakes, 8 to 10 minutes. (Do not overcook.) Discard any mussels that don't open.

Mound the couscous in the center of a large, shallow serving platter. Arrange the carrot, turnip, and zucchini sticks atop the couscous like spokes of a wheel. Set the fish, shellfish, and peppers around the dish. Ladle some of the hot broth over the couscous. Serve immediately, with harissa and remaining soup broth on the side.

MARQA DEL HOOT
Fish Stock

Makes 8 cups

5 or 6 fish heads (purchased from a fish monger or Asian markets)
8   cups water
2   bay leaves
1   onion studded with 4 cloves
8   peppercorns
1   cup dry white wine
30 fresh flat-leaf parsley sprigs, tied with cotton string
8   celery stalks with leaves or 8 fennel fronds
Salt to taste

In a large soup pot, combine the fish heads, water, bay leaves, clove-studded onion, peppercorns, wine, parsley, and celery. Cover and simmer for 1 to 1 ½ hours. Using a slotted spoon, periodically skim off the foam. Strain through a fine-meshed sieve. Season with salt to taste and refrigerate until ready to use.

K'SEKSOO B'KEMROON
Couscous Timbales with Shrimp

Serves 6

The fresh shrimp I purchase at the port city of El Jadida, just five miles down the road from Azemmour, inspired these flavorful timbales. Serve them at room temperature.

Red Pepper Coulis:

2 red bell peppers, roasted, peeled, and seeded (see page 33)

½ cup chicken broth

1 garlic clove, minced

2 teaspoons fresh lemon juice

Timbales:

3 tablespoons olive oil

1 teaspoon sweet Hungarian paprika

½ teaspoon ground cumin

2 garlic cloves, minced

8 ounces medium shrimp, shelled and deveined

1 to 1½ cups chicken broth

1½ cups instant couscous

1 red bell pepper, seeded, deribbed, and finely diced

¼ cup minced fresh cilantro

3 inner celery stalks, finely diced

2 teaspoons finely diced Preserved Lemon rind (page 36)

3 tablespoons fresh lemon juice

Freshly ground pepper to taste

6 fresh cilantro leaves for garnish

To make the coulis: In a blender or food processor, combine the roasted peppers, chicken broth, and garlic. Process to a smooth puree. Season with lemon juice. Set aside.

To make the timbales: In a medium skillet over medium-high heat, heat 2 tablespoons of the olive oil. Add the paprika, cumin, and garlic. Cook, stirring, until fragrant, 1 to 2 minutes. Add the shrimp and cook until they turn pink, 3 to 4 minutes. With a slotted spoon, transfer the shrimp to a cutting board and cut them into ½-inch dice. Set aside.

Transfer the pan juices to a measuring cup. Add enough chicken broth to make 1½ cups liquid. In a medium saucepan, bring the liquid to a boil with the remaining 1 tablespoon olive oil. Gradually stir in the couscous and remove from the heat. Cover and let stand for 5 minutes. Transfer the couscous to a bowl and fluff with a fork. Let cool. Add half the diced pepper, the cilantro, celery, lemon rind, lemon juice, ground pepper, and diced shrimp. Set aside.

Pack ⅔-cup portions of the couscous mixture into 6 slightly oiled ramekins. Unmold the timbales on salad plates, and spoon some coulis around the base of each. Garnish with diced red pepper and a cilantro leaf.

K'SEKSOO MITIDJA

Chicken Couscous with Raisins, Almonds, and Pine Nuts

Serves 6

My friend Danielle Carceles-Charrié grew up in the northeastern Moroccan city of Oujda. The following recipe is typical of that region, and one of her family's favorites.

2 tablespoons olive oil

3 pounds chicken pieces

4 onions, thinly sliced

3 garlic cloves, minced

4 tomatoes, seeded and coarsely cubed

3 red bell peppers, seeded, deribbed, and quartered lengthwise

10 fresh cilantro sprigs, tied with cotton string

20 fresh flat-leaf parsley sprigs, tied with cotton string

1 teaspoon ground ginger

¾ teaspoon ground cloves

¼ teaspoon freshly grated nutmeg

1 teaspoon ground cinnamon

10 threads Spanish saffron, toasted and crushed (see page 32)

1 teaspoon ground turmeric

10 cups water

1 cup golden raisins

¼ cup pine nuts, toasted (see page 33)

Salt and freshly ground pepper to taste

2 tablespoons butter

2 cups instant couscous

½ cup whole blanched almonds, toasted (see page 33)

Harissa (page 39), for serving

In a large soup pot over medium-high heat, heat the olive oil and cook the chicken, stirring occasionally, until it turns golden, 3 to 4 minutes. Add the onions, garlic, tomatoes, peppers, cilantro, parsley, ginger, cloves, nutmeg, cinnamon, saffron, turmeric, and 8 cups of the water. Cover and simmer until the chicken is tender, 40 to 45 minutes.

Preheat the oven to 200 degrees F. With a slotted spoon, transfer the chicken and the peppers to an ovenproof dish. Cover and keep warm. Discard the cilantro and parsley. Add the raisins and half of the pine nuts to the soup pot. Season with salt and pepper.

In a medium saucepan, bring the remaining 2 cups water and the butter to a boil. Gradually stir in the couscous and remove from the heat. Cover and let stand for 5 minutes. Add ¼ cup soup broth and fluff with a fork.

To serve, mound the couscous in the center of a large platter. Garnish with the toasted almonds and remaining pine nuts. Arrange the chicken and the peppers around the base of the couscous. Serve with soup broth and harissa on the side.

SEFFA
Sweet Cinnamon Couscous with Dried Fruit

The sweet couscous called *seffa* is a dessert reserved for special occasions. It calls for the finest grade of couscous, which is steamed several times to obtain light and fluffy granules. I often use seffa as an accompaniment for roast meats. The following adaptation is also a favorite stuffing for our family's Thanksgiving turkey.

Makes 3 cups

4 tablespoons butter

2 shallots, minced

1 cup chicken broth

6 threads Spanish saffron, crushed

1 cup instant couscous

2 tablespoons sugar

1 tablespoon orange-flower water (see page 31)

1 teaspoon ground cinnamon

2 tablespoons raisins, plumped in warm water and drained

4 dates, pitted and chopped

6 dried apricot halves, plumped in warm water, drained, and diced

2 tablespoons slivered almonds, toasted (see page 33)

Salt and freshly ground pepper to taste

In a medium saucepan over medium heat, melt 2 tablespoons of the butter and add the shallots. Sauté until the shallots are translucent, 2 to 3 minutes. Add the broth, saffron, and remaining 2 tablespoons butter. Bring to a boil. Gradually stir in the couscous and remove from the heat. Cover and let stand for 5 minutes.

Transfer the couscous to a bowl and fluff with a fork. Stir in the sugar, orange-flower water, cinnamon, raisins, dates, apricots, and slivered almonds. Season with salt and pepper. Use as a stuffing, or serve hot as a side dish.

MECHROOBAT

WA

HALAWIYET

Beverages and Desserts

It would be hard to imagine any Moroccan getting through the day without several glasses of *atay b'nahna*, or mint tea.

Green tea first came to the court of Sultan Moulay Ismael in 1721, when England's King George I, eager to open up trade with Morocco, sent him several bales of tea as a gift. At some point, generous quantities of mint leaves and sugar were combined with the Chinese green tea to create a new drink that would become wildly popular. Author James Grey Jackson, Esq., relates in *Account of the Empire of Morocco* that during the first seven months of 1806, British traders unloaded 1,310 pounds of green tea at the port of Mogador (now Essaouira). From there, the bales were transported by camel caravans to the heart of the empire. Green tea didn't become widely used, however, until the mid-1850s, when British merchants were forced to seek new markets for their exports because of a blockade of the Baltic Sea during the Crimean War.

The preparation and serving of mint tea has since become a social tradition observed throughout Morocco, from modest shepherds' huts to the most lavish villas in Casablanca. Custom dictates that guests sip three glasses of the fragrant beverage before taking their leave. Every household owns a *siniya,* an ornate, three-legged tray that holds the implements and ingredients necessary for preparing mint tea: a *berrad,* a pot-bellied silver teapot; decoratively painted glasses; and several ornate boxes containing tea, chunks of sugar loaf, and leaves of fresh spearmint.

The host is responsible for preparing and serving mint tea. He expertly pours the sweet beverage into small glasses—sometimes from a height of several feet—in order to aerate the brew and demonstrate his skill. Anyone who has spent time in Moroccan bazaars knows the importance of mint tea to the conducting of delicate negotiations. Mint tea is usually served at the end of the meal with dessert, or anytime sweets are offered.

ATAY B'NAHNA
Mint Tea

Morocco's national drink is made with Chinese green tea such as Gunpowder or young Hyson. Neither black tea nor Japanese green tea are used in atay b'nahna.

To the tea, Moroccans add fresh spearmint and generous amounts of sugar. Additional ingredients may also be included to flavor the tea. In the saffron-growing region of Taliouine, for instance, the local Berbers add a liberal quantity of saffron to the pot. They believe the resulting amber-colored beverage has life-extending properties. In other parts of Morocco, fresh orange blossoms, leaves of lemon verbena, aniseed, cinnamon sticks, or a sprig of absinthe may be added to the fragrant brew.

**Makes
5 cups**

2   teaspoons Chinese green tea

5   cups boiling water

½   cup sugar

15   fresh spearmint sprigs

Fresh orange blossoms, 1 sprig lemon verbena, 6 aniseeds,
   or one 2-inch cinnamon stick (optional)

In a teapot, combine the tea and the boiling water. Let steep for 2 minutes. Add the sugar, mint, and any of the optional ingredients. Let stand for 3 to 4 minutes. Serve immediately.

Note: To order fine Chinese green teas, see Mail-Order Sources, page 150. Mint tea is also delicious served over ice.

HLIB B'LOUZ
Sweet Almond Milk

Serves 4

Try this unusual and refreshing drink on a hot summer afternoon. In Morocco, it accompanies a small plate of dates and is offered to honored guests as a sign of welcome.

2   **cups whole milk**

½   **cup sugar**

2   **cups whole blanched almonds**

2   **cups water**

2   **tablespoons orange-flower water**
    (see page 31)

Fresh mint sprigs for garnish

In a medium saucepan, bring the milk and sugar to a boil over medium-high heat. Stir until the sugar dissolves. Remove from the heat and let cool.

In a blender, process 1 cup of the milk with the almonds on high speed until the nuts are finely ground. Strain through a fine-meshed sieve and press with the back of a large spoon to extract as much liquid as possible. Discard the almond residue. Add the remaining milk, the water and orange-flower water, and stir. Serve over ice cubes and garnish with a sprig of mint.

SELLOH

Toasted Flour and Almond Confections

Selloh, a sweetened blend of toasted flour, ground sesame seeds, and ground almonds, is reputed for its fortifying quality. For this reason, it is given to mothers after childbirth. It is also a popular midnight snack during the holy month of Ramadan. Moroccan cooks traditionally present selloh mounded on a platter. I prefer to serve them in the shape of truffles, set in individual fluted paper cups.

Makes about 40 to 45 confections

1 cup all-purpose flour

½ cup whole-wheat flour

1 teaspoon ground cinnamon

½ cup powdered sugar

1¼ cups whole blanched almonds, toasted (see page 33)

1 cup (about 6 ounces) unhulled sesame seeds, toasted (see page 33)

2 tablespoons aniseed, toasted (see page 33)

2 tablespoons honey

½ cup plus 2 tablespoons unsalted butter, melted

Powdered sugar for coating

½ cup slivered almonds, toasted (see page 33), for garnish

In a large cast-iron skillet over medium-high heat, toast the all-purpose and whole-wheat flours together in batches, stirring frequently, until they emit a pleasant toasted aroma and turn lightly golden, 10 to 12 minutes. Transfer to a large bowl. Stir in the cinnamon and the sugar. Set aside.

In a food processor, finely grind the almonds, sesame seeds, and aniseed. Add to the flour mixture. Stir in the honey and butter. Mix well with your hands.

Roll 2 teaspoons of the mixture between your palms to make balls 1 to 1¼ inches in diameter. Roll them in powdered sugar and set them in fluted paper cups. Garnish each with a slivered almond and serve. Selloh keep well for up to 2 weeks in an airtight container in the refrigerator.

HASSIR ROMMAN B'LIMMOUN
Fresh Pomegranate and Orange Juice

Many gardens in Morocco include at least one pomegranate bush. The ruby-red seeds of the *romman,* as the fruit is known in Arabic, are usually eaten out of hand. Sometimes, Moroccan mothers welcome their children home from school with a refreshing glass of pomegranate-orange drink.

Serves 1

1   **pomegranate**
¼   **cup water**
½   **cup fresh orange juice**
Sugar to taste
2   **teaspoons orange-flower water**
      (see page 31)
Fresh mint sprigs for garnish

Fill a large bowl with water. Cut the pomegranate in half lengthwise. Holding the fruit under the water, break it apart, separating the seeds from the skin and white pith. The seeds will drop to the bottom of the bowl, while the pith will float to the surface. Transfer the seeds to a colander or strainer. Rinse, removing any remaining bits of skin and pith.

In a blender or a juicer, puree the pomegranate seeds with the water. Strain through a fine-meshed sieve, pressing the puree with the back of a large spoon to extract as much liquid as possible. Transfer to a container and stir in the orange juice, sugar, and orange-flower water. Serve over ice cubes and garnish with a mint sprig.

KA'AB AL GHAZAL
Gazelle Horns

Thirteenth-century Andalusian jurist and cookbook author Ibn Razin al-Tudjibi called these crescent-shaped almond-paste delicacies "gazelle hoofs." Seven hundred years later, in the early 1900s, British author Budgett Meakin gave this advice to his readers: "If you are wise, you will most assuredly try the 'gazelle's hoofs,' so-called from their shape, for they are a most delicious compound of almond paste, with a spiciness so skillfully blended as to be almost elusive." Today, though the name has changed to "gazelle horns," the recipe remains the same.

Makes about 40 pastries

Almond Paste:

1   **pound slivered blanched almonds**

¾   **cup powdered sugar**

3½ **tablespoons unsalted butter, melted**

⅛   **teaspoon almond extract**

2   **tablespoons orange-flower water (see page 31)**

Dough:

2   **cups all-purpose flour**

½   **teaspoon salt**

4   **tablespoons unsalted butter, melted**

½   **cup orange-flower water (see page 31)**

1   **tablespoon water**

1   **egg**

1   **tablespoon water**

Powdered sugar for coating

To make the almond paste: In a grain mill, meat grinder, spice grinder, or food processor, grind the almonds 3 or 4 times until they achieve an almost pastelike consistency. Transfer them to a large bowl. Add the remaining almond paste ingredients. With your hands, blend the mixture thoroughly to obtain a thick, sticky dough. Cover with plastic wrap to prevent it from drying out. Set aside.

To make the dough: In a large mixing bowl, sift the flour with the salt and make a well in the center. Stir in the butter, orange-flower water, and 1 tablespoon of water. On a lightly floured board, knead by hand until the dough is smooth and elastic, 10 to 12 minutes. Set aside for 15 minutes.

Preheat the oven to 325 degrees F. Divide the dough into 4 equal parts. On a floured work surface, roll out one part to an 8-by-10-inch rectangle. Trim the edges to make them even and cut the rectangle into 10 rectangles, each 2 by 4 inches. Take 1 heaping tablespoon of almond paste and, with your hands, form it into a 4-inch-long spindle. Set it on one of the rectangles. Fold over and seal the edges of the dough with the tines of a fork. Trim the edges with a knife or a pastry wheel. Carefully shape the pastry into a crescent. Make a ridge along the top by pinching the dough between the thumb and forefinger. With a toothpick, pierce the pastry in 4 or 5 places. Repeat to fill and shape the remaining rectangles, then repeat the process with the remaining 3 parts of dough. (Wrap any remaining almond paste tightly with plastic wrap, and keep refrigerated. Use within 5 to 6 months.)

In a small bowl, make an egg wash by beating the egg with the other 1 tablespoon of water. With a pastry brush, paint each gazelle horn with the mixture and place on a parchment-lined or nonstick baking sheet. Bake in the center of the oven until lightly golden but not brown, 8 to 10 minutes. Let cool a few minutes. Roll in powdered sugar. Serve warm or at room temperature.

BRIOUAT BIL FAKIYA
Dried-Fruit Briouats

Makes 15 to 18 briouats

These lovely honey-drenched briouats are filled with a rich dried-fruit mixture called *fakiya*, which is meant to symbolize prosperity.

8 dried apricot halves	1 cup fresh orange juice
8 dried apple slices	½ teaspoon ground cinnamon
½ cup seedless raisins	5 sheets phyllo dough, thawed
1 cup walnut halves, toasted (see page 33)	Vegetable oil for frying
12 pitted dates	1 cup honey

In separate small bowls, soak the apricots, apples, and raisins in warm water to cover until plump, about 20 minutes. Drain.

In a blender or food processor, combine the walnuts, dates, apricots, and apples. Process until coarsely ground. Transfer to a large bowl. Add the raisins, half the orange juice, and the cinnamon. Mix well. Set aside.

Set the stacked phyllo on a work surface. With the long edge of the phyllo toward you, and using a sharp knife, cut through the stacked sheets of dough to make 4 equal sections, each about 4 ½ inches wide. Work with 1 strip of phyllo at a time, keeping the rest of the phyllo covered with a damp towel. Place 1 tablespoon of the filling about 1 inch from the bottom edge of the strip. Fold a corner of the strip over the filling so the bottom edge is flush with the long edge. Continue folding, as you would a flag, to obtain a triangular shape. Use the beaten egg to seal the free edge. Repeat the process until all the filling has been used.

In a heavy, medium saucepan, pour the oil to a depth of 2 inches. Heat it until it reaches 325 degrees F, or until a piece of phyllo dropped into it sizzles instantly. Fry the briouats in batches until golden, about 6 to 8 minutes. Using a slotted spoon, transfer to paper towels to drain.

In a small saucepan, bring the honey and the remaining orange juice to a low boil. With tongs, immediately dip each briouat into the boiling mixture until well coated. Set aside on a serving platter. Serve at room temperature.

Note: These briouats will keep for up to 1 week in an airtight container in the refrigerator. Bring them to room temperature before serving.

GHORIBA
Sesame Cookies

**Makes
4 dozen
cookies**

Naïma Lakhmar, a professional caterer in Azemmour, makes *ghoriba* (pronounced "greeba") by the hundreds for special celebrations. Because she is used to working with such large quantities of ingredients, Naïma is amused whenever she sees me carefully filling my relatively small American cups and tablespoons.

¾ **cup (about 4½ ounces) unhulled
  sesame seeds, toasted (see page 33)**
3 **cups unbleached all-purpose flour**
1 **teaspoon baking powder**
1½ **cups powdered sugar**
4 **tablespoons butter at room temperature**
¾ **cup plus 2 tablespoons vegetable oil**
Powdered sugar for sprinkling

In a wide, shallow bowl, mix the sesame seeds, flour, baking powder, 1¼ cups of the powdered sugar, and the butter. Gradually add the oil, stirring vigorously, to make a dough. Turn the dough out onto a lightly floured board and knead until smooth and elastic. This could take up to 10 minutes. Let the dough rest for 20 to 30 minutes.

Preheat the oven to 350 degrees F. Take 1 tablespoon of the dough and, with your hands, roll it into a 1-inch ball. Set it on a greased or nonstick baking sheet and flatten it with your fingers to 1½ inches in diameter. Continue in this manner until all the dough is used.

Bake until the cookies turn light brown, 12 to 15 minutes. Let cool slightly on the baking sheet, then, with a metal spatula, transfer them to a wire rack. Sprinkle with the remaining powdered sugar and serve.

HALOUA TPOLO
Chocolate Sesame Cones

Makes about 3 dozen cones

"The name *tpolo* actually refers to a popular brand of ice cream," explains my friend Naïma, who taught me how to make these unusual cone-shaped cookies. Because making tpolo is a labor-intensive proposition, you may want to recruit an assistant for the task.

Cones:

1   cup (about 6 ounces) unhulled sesame seeds, toasted (see page 33)

1   cup all-purpose flour

¼   teaspoon baking powder

1   egg yolk, lightly beaten

¼   cup orange-flower water (see page 31)

2   tablespoons butter, melted

1   tablespoon vegetable oil, plus vegetable oil for deep-frying

2   cups honey

Filling:

⅓   cup semisweet chocolate chips

2   tablespoons butter

½   cup sweet condensed milk

½   cup slivered blanched almonds, toasted and coarsely ground (see page 33)

To make the cones: In a large, shallow bowl, mix the sesame seeds, flour, and baking powder until well blended. Make a well in the center and add the egg yolk, orange-flower water, butter, and 1 tablespoon vegetable oil. Mix these ingredients into the flour mixture until well blended.

Turn the dough out onto a lightly floured board and knead vigorously until smooth and elastic, 8 to 10 minutes. If the dough is too dry, add 1 to 2 tablespoons water and knead again until it stretches easily. Shape the dough into a large ball and let it rest for 10 minutes.

Separate the dough into 4 equal parts. Cover the portions with plastic wrap to prevent them from drying out. On a lightly floured board, roll each ball of dough out to a ⅛-inch thickness. With a 2 ½-inch-diameter cookie cutter, cut out circles of dough. Wrap each circle around the end of your index finger to form a cone. Seal the tip and make sure the sides stick together. Set the cones gently on a parchment-lined baking sheet, making sure they don't touch.

In a large, heavy saucepan over medium heat, heat 2 inches of the oil to 280 degrees F or until a piece of dough sizzles instantly. Deep-fry the cones in small batches (see Notes). They will sink, then float back to the surface. Fry until pale golden, 3 to 4 minutes. Using tongs, care-

(continued)

fully set the cones upright in between the grids of a wire rack set over paper towels to drain (or set the cones upright along the inside walls of a large container lined with paper towels).

In a heavy, medium saucepan, bring the honey to a boil. Using tongs, dip each cone into the boiling honey. Return the cones to the rack or container to cool, keeping them separate from one another.

To make the filling: Place a medium saucepan inside a large skillet filled with lightly simmering water. To the pan, add the chocolate, butter, and condensed milk. Stir constantly until the chocolate is melted and shiny (see Notes). Remove from heat and stir in the ground almonds.

Carefully fill each cone with some of the warm chocolate mixture. Set the filled cones upright in between the grids of the wire rack or the inside wall of the large container and refrigerate until the filling hardens, 1 to 1 ½ hours. To store, layer the cookies in an airtight container, separating each layer with parchment paper.

The cookies will keep for 2 months in the refrigerator. Bring them back to room temperature before serving.

Notes: To avoid excessive foaming while deep-frying the cones, set a stainless steel teaspoon in the oil at the bottom of the pan. It works!

If the chocolate hardens and turns grainy, your water temperature is too high. To remedy that, remove the chocolate from the heat, add 1 teaspoon water, and stir vigorously. Continue adding water 1 teaspoon at a time and stirring until you get a shiny glaze. Use immediately.

TMAR B'LOOZ
Dates with Almond Paste Filling

Dates are a staple of the North African diet. During the Moslem observance of Ramadan, they traditionally accompany the first bowl of harira soup that breaks the day's fast. In Moroccan homes, dates are a common item on the dessert tray, along with other dried fruits, fresh fruits, and nuts. Occasionally, they are served stuffed with almond paste tinted with green food coloring (green is believed to have been the Prophet Mohammed's favorite color). The best dates for stuffing are plump Medjools, a variety native to the oases of the Moroccan and Algerian Sahara. Fortunately, they are also grown in California's Coachella Valley, near Palm Springs (see Mail-Order Sources for fresh Medjools). Commercial almond paste is available in the baking section of supermarkets, or you can make your own.

**Makes
24 dates**

⅔ cup (7 ounces) almond paste (see page 136)

1 tablespoon orange-flower water (see page 31)

3 drops green food coloring (optional)

24 dates, preferably Medjools, sliced open (not cut in half) and pitted

Grated zest of 1 orange

In a medium bowl, using your fingers, thoroughly mix the almond paste with the orange-flower water and the optional food coloring. Form 1 heaping teaspoon of almond paste into a spindle shape and stuff the paste into the date. Lightly compress the date to force the almond paste to bulge out slightly. Repeat to fill all the dates. Set the dates on a platter and garnish with the orange zest.

Note: Stuffed dates will keep for up to 3 months in an airtight container in the refrigerator. Bring them back to room temperature before serving.

KTEFFA

Phyllo Pastries with Orange-Flower Custard and Fresh Berries

Makes 6 pastries

Kteffa is an elegant dessert served in some of Morocco's most exclusive restaurants. Traditionally, large, circular sheets of ouarka are deep-fried, layered with ground almonds, sugar, and cinnamon, and covered with warm custard. In this variation, individual pastries are baked, smothered in custard, and garnished with fresh berries.

1¾ cups whole blanched almonds, toasted (see page 33)

¼ cup powdered sugar

2 teaspoons ground cinnamon

8 sheets phyllo dough, thawed

½ cup (1 stick butter), melted

2 cups milk

¼ cup granulated sugar

1 cinnamon stick

3 tablespoons cornstarch

1 cup heavy cream

2 tablespoons orange-flower water (see page 31)

2 cups fresh raspberries, blackberries, or strawberries for garnish

Preheat the oven to 350 degrees F. In a blender or food processor, coarsely grind the almonds. Transfer to a medium bowl and combine them with the powdered sugar and cinnamon. Set aside.

Stack the phyllo sheets on a work surface. Using a sharp knife, with a 4-inch-diameter bowl or saucer as a template, cut 6 circles in the stacked phyllo. You will have 48 phyllo circles, or 8 for each pastry. Discard the scraps.

On a parchment-lined or nonstick baking sheet, stack 2 phyllo leaves, lightly brushing each with melted butter. Sprinkle the top leaf evenly with 1 level tablespoon of the ground almond mixture. Repeat this process twice. Top with 2 final buttered leaves. Repeat this entire process to make the remaining 5 pastries.

Bake the pastries on the center rack of the oven until golden brown, 20 to 25 minutes. Remove from the oven and, with a metal spatula, transfer each pastry to a dessert plate.

In a medium saucepan, bring the milk, sugar, and cinnamon stick to a simmer over medium heat. In a small bowl, whisk the cornstarch into the cream. Add this mixture to the simmering milk, along with the orange-flower water. Cook, stirring, until the orange flower custard mixture coats the spoon. Discard the cinnamon stick. Pour ½ cup of warm custard over each pastry, garnish with berries, and serve immediately.

MOOTTELEJ DEL BOORTOOKAL LA MAMOUNIA

Orange-Cinnamon Sherbet La Mamounia

As a child, I can recall spending a weekend with my family at the La Mamounia Hotel in Marrakesh, considered even then to be one of the world's most luxurious hotels. Winston Churchill, a Mamounia habitué in his latter years, devoted many hours to painting in the hotel's lovely rose gardens. Today, executive chef Boujemaa Mars, a member of the hotel's kitchen staff for more than twenty-five years, prepares this delightfully refreshing sherbet. The word *sherbet* itself is derived from the Arabic *charab,* meaning to drink. Although it was invented by the Chinese, the refreshing dessert was adopted by the Persians and Turks, who later introduced it throughout the Mediterranean Basin.

Serves 6

2¾ cups fresh orange juice, strained

⅓ cup fresh lemon juice, strained

2 cinnamon sticks

¼ cup sugar

1 tablespoon orange-flower water (see page 31)

2 oranges

Ground cinnamon for garnish

Grated orange zest for garnish

In a medium saucepan, combine the orange juice, lemon juice, cinnamon sticks, and sugar. Cook over medium heat, stirring, until the sugar dissolves, 5 to 6 minutes. Remove from heat and add the orange-flower water. Let stand for 1 to 2 hours.

Discard the cinnamon sticks. Pour the mixture into 6 individual molds. Freeze until firm. With a large, sharp knife, cut off the top and bottom of the oranges down to the flesh. Set the oranges on end and cut off the peel down to the flesh. Cut the oranges into ¼-inch slices. Cut each slice in half and remove the seeds. Set aside.

To serve, unmold each sherbet onto individual dessert plates and surround with halved orange slices. Lightly sprinkle the fruit with cinnamon. Garnish with orange zest. Serve immediately.

K'SEKSOO B'ROMMAN WA L'BEN

Sweet Pomegranate Couscous
with Buttermilk

I prepare this dessert as soon as pomegranates make their late-summer appearance at the Azemmour souk. I generously blend the "tears of the Prophet," as Moroccans call the ruby-colored seeds, with sweetened couscous. Traditionally, a glass of *lben,* a kind of buttermilk, accompanies sweet couscous. For this variation, however, I prefer to serve couscous and buttermilk together in the same bowl.

Serves 6

1   **ripe pomegranate**

1   **cup water**

½   **teaspoon salt**

1   **cup instant couscous**

2   **tablespoons sugar**

Buttermilk for serving

Fresh mint leaves for garnish

Fill a large bowl with water. Cut the pomegranate in half lengthwise. Holding the fruit under water, break it apart, separating the seeds from the outer skin and white pith. The seeds will drop to the bottom of the bowl, and the pith will float to the surface. Pour the seeds into a colander or strainer. Rinse, removing any remaining bits of skin and pith.

In a small saucepan, bring the water and salt to a boil. Gradually stir in the couscous and remove from the heat. Cover and let stand for 5 minutes. Transfer to a large bowl. Add the sugar and pomegranate seeds, and mix thoroughly. Pack a small ramekin with the couscous mixture and invert it in a shallow soup bowl. Pour a little buttermilk around the base of the couscous. Garnish with mint leaves and serve.

Menus

A Family-Style Dinner

Assortment of salads

Kefta Mahchiya (Stuffed Meatballs with Dried Fruit in Sweet Onion Sauce)

Hobz Belboula (Barley Bread with Cumin)

Seasonal fruit

Atay b'Nahna (Mint Tea), fresh fruit juices, or mineral water

Another Family-Style Dinner

Zahlouk (Cooked Eggplant and Tomato Salad)

Loubia (Four-Spice Lamb and Bean Soup)

Hobz Belboula (Barley Bread with Cumin)

K'seksoo b'Romman wa L'ben (Sweet Pomegranate Couscous with Buttermilk)

Atay b'Nahna (Mint Tea)

Friday Lunch

Assortment of salads

K'seksoo Beïdaoui (Couscous Casablanca Style)

Harissa (North African Hot Sauce)

Seasonal fruit

Briouat bil Fakiya (Dried-Fruit Briouats)

Atay b'Nahna (Mint Tea), fresh fruit juices, or mineral water

A Celebration Dinner

Assortment of salads

Mechoui (Leg of Lamb with Preserved Lemon, Olive Oil, Garlic, and Cumin Marinade)

Hobz Belboula (Barley Bread with Cumin)

Moottelej del Boortookal La Mamounia (Orange-Cinnamon Sherbet La Mamounia)

Ghoriba (Sesame Cookies)

Atay b'Nahna (Mint Tea), fresh fruit juices, or mineral water

A Moroccan Picnic

Sebha del Hdaree (Ratatouille with Dates)

Meslalla (Orange and Olive Salad)

Chlada b'Felfla wa L'hamd Markad (Roasted Pepper, Preserved Lemon, and Parsley Salad)

Al Kotban Mrakchiya (Shish Kabobs Marrakesh Style)

Harissa (North African Hot Sauce)

Hobz Belboula (Barley Bread with Cumin)

Seasonal fruit

Fresh fruit juices or mineral water

Breaking the Fast of Ramadan

Café au lait

Kraiychlet (Anise and Sesame Seed Buns)

Harira (Ramadan Soup of Fava Beans and Lentils)

Dates

Hard-boiled eggs

Hobz Belboula (Barley Bread with Cumin)

Selloh (Toasted Flour and Almond Confections)

Seasonal fruit

Fresh fruit juices, milk, or buttermilk

A Sephardic Dinner

Chorba del Fool Treh (Passover Fava Bean Soup with Fresh Coriander)

Dafina (Sephardic Sabbath Stew)

L'Hass b'Limmoun wa Tmar (Hearts of Romaine, Orange, and Date Salad)

Tmar b'Looz (Dates with Almond Paste Filling)

Kteffa (Phyllo Pastries with Orange-Flower Custard and Fresh Berries)

Coffee, wine, or mineral water

A Moroccan Tea

Fresh fruit juices, whole milk, buttermilk

Café au lait

Atay b'Nahna (Mint Tea)

Kraiychlet (Anise and Sesame Seed Buns)

Ka'ab al Ghazal (Gazelle Horns), *Ghoriba* (Sesame Cookies), or *Haloua Tpolo* (Chocolate Sesame Cones)

Dates, dried figs, almonds, and walnuts

Bibliography

Ayache, Albert. *Histoire ancienne de l'Afrique du Nord.* Paris: Editions Sociales, 1964.

Bloom, Carole. *The International Dictionary of Desserts, Pastries, and Confections.* New York: Hearst Books, 1995.

Brunot, Louis. *Au Seuil de la vie marocaine.* Casablanca: Librairie Farairre, 1950.

Champion, Honoré, éd. *Villes et tribus du Maroc, région des Doukkalas, Azemmour et sa banlieue.* Vol. 9. Paris: Documents et Renseignements Publiés par la Direction des Affaires Indigènes, 1932.

Charlesworth, M. P. *Trade-Routes and Commerce of the Roman Empire.* 2nd rev. ed. Chicago: Ares Publishers, 1974.

Chraïbi, Driss. *La Mère du printemps (Oum-er-Bia).* Paris: Editions du Seuil, 1982.

Cunninghame Graham, R. B. *Mogreb-El-Acksa: A Journey in Morocco.* New York: National Travel Club, 1930.

Drummond Hay, John H. *Western Barbary: Its Wild Tribes and Savage Animals.* London: John Murray, Albemarle Street, n.d.

Facciola, Stephen. *Cornucopia: A Sourcebook of Edible Plants.* Vista, CA.: Kampong Publications, 1990.

Guinaudeau-Franc, Zette. *Fès vu par sa cuisine.* Rabat: Editions J. E. Laurent, 1957.

Jackson, G. James. *An Account of the Empire of Morocco and the District of Suse, Compiled from Miscellaneous Observations Made during a Long Residence in, and Various Journeys through Those Countries.* Philadelphia: Fry and Kammerer, 1810.

Lakhal, Naïma. "La Production et la consommation de couscous au Maroc: de l'artisanat à l'industrie." Ph.D. diss., University of Toulouse-Le Mirail, 1988. Available from the author at B.P. 83, El Jadida Principale, Morocco.

Loti, Pierre. *Morocco.* New York: Frederick A. Stockes, 1889.

Meakin, Budgett. *Life in Morocco and Glimpses Beyond.* London: Chatto & Windus, 1905.

Messaoudi, Leïla et Mohamed. *L'Art de vivre marocain: Traditions et coutumes des communautés musulmanes et juives.* Paris: Eddif International, 1981.

Morse, Kitty. *Come with Me to the Kasbah: A Cook's Tour of Morocco.* Casablanca: SERAR, 1989.

————. *The Vegetarian Table: North Africa.* San Francisco: Chronicle Books, 1996.

Pellow, Thomas. *The Adventures of Thomas Pellow, of Penryn, Mariner: Three and Twenty Years in Captivity Among the Moors Written by Himself.* London: T. Fisher Unwin, 1890.

Perry, Charles. "Buran: 1100 Years in the Life of a Dish." *The Journal of Gastronomy 1* (1984).

Roget, Raymond. *Le Maroc chez les auteurs anciens.* Paris: Société d'Edition les Belles Lettres, 1924.

Sijelmassi, Abdelhaii. *Les Plantes médicinales du Maroc.* 2d ed. Casablanca: Editions le Fennec, 1991.

Westermarck, Edward. *Ritual and Belief in Morocco,* vol. I. London: MacMillan and Co. Limited, 1926.

Mail-Order Sources

Cornwall Bridge Pottery
Route 128
West Cornwall, CT 06796
(800) 501-6545

Lead-free Moroccan tagine dishes made to order.

Greater Galilee Gourmet, Inc.
2118 Wilshire Boulevard, Suite 829
Santa Monica, CA 90403
(800) 290-1391

Olives and olive oils from the Middle East and North Africa.

Kalustyan Orient Export Co.
123 Lexington Avenue
New York, NY 10016
(212) 685-3451

Spices. Couscoussières.

MSE Enterprises Inc.
2522 Corte Bella
Pleasanton, CA 94566
(510) 220-0084

Decorative pottery, teapots, tea glasses, and tagine dishes.

Nick Sciabica & Sons
P.O. Box 1246
Modesto, CA 95353
(800) 551-9612

Olive oil.

Nomads of Santa Fe
207 Shelby Street
Santa Fe, NM 87501
(800) 360-4807

Moroccan imports, including tagine dishes.

Northwestern Coffee Mills
217 North Broadway
Milwaukee, WI 53202
(800) 243-5283

Fine coffees and teas (including Chinese young Hyson tea).

Oasis Date Gardens
59-111 Highway 111
P.O. Box 757
Thermal, CA 92274
(800) 827-8017

Dates.

Oasis Naturals
P.O. Box 12871
La Jolla, CA 92039
(619) 276-1440

Dried harissa powder and other North African spice blends.

The Spice House
103 North Old World Third Street
Milwaukee, WI 53203
(414) 272-0977 and
1941 Central Street
Evanston, IL 60201
(847) 328-3711

Spices (including ras el hanout).

Vanns Spices Ltd.
1238 Joppa Road
Baltimore, MD 21286
(410) 583-1643

Spices.

Volubilis Imports
P.O. Box 2393
San Diego, CA 92038
(888) VOLUBILIS

Importer of Moroccan wines.

Wunderley Imports
93 Northmont Street
Greensburg, PA 15601
(724) 850-9616

Moroccan artifacts, teapots, and decorative pottery.

Acknowledgments

My thanks to longtime family friends Aziz and Nadia Belkasmi of Casablanca; Naïma Bounaïm, a former resident of Dar Zitoun whose personal reminiscences added so much to the spirit of this book; noted artist Salah Eddine Chaoui and his wife, Zineb, of Marrakesh; Mehdi Illane and Brahim Mahdi, owner and chef of l'Hippocampe restaurant in Oualidia; economist Naïma Lakhal, Ph.D., an expert in all matters pertaining to couscous; Zemmouri caterer Naïma Lakhmar, in whose company I spent many enjoyable hours in the kitchen of Dar Zitoun; architect Abdel Ila Lemseffer and his wife, Ahlam, a well-known painter; Jacques and Danielle Mamane of Fez; executive chef Boujemaa Mars of La Mamounia Hotel in Marrakesh; historian Guy Martinet; Bouchaïb Marzouk, for more than three decades our housekeeper at Dar Zitoun (a superb cook in his own right), and his wife, Aïcha; prominent ceramist Abderrahmane Rahoule and his wife, Roseline; Zemmouri neighbors Mohamed Rahmoun and his sister, Rachida; archaeologist and author Susan Searight; and linguist and anthropologist Abderrahim Youssi, Ph.D., of Mohammed V University in Rabat.

In the United States, I would like to thank friends and colleagues Carole Bloom, Tershia d'Elgin, Edith Fine, Wendy Haskett, and Judith Josephson for their support and encouragement; food writer Stella Fong for her help during the photo shoot; Professor Fakhereddine Berrada, Mohamed El Mandjra, and Aziza Rharrit for their linguistic assistance; *Los Angeles Times* staff writer and food historian Charles Perry; Dick and Margo Baughman, and Andrea Peterson, who kept me supplied with fresh figs and pomegranates.

I thank my mother, Nicole Darmon Chandler, my aunt, Martine Darmon Meyer, and my cousin, Flor Scemama, as well as our friends Jim and Froukje Frost, whose knowledge of Moroccan cuisine was of precious help in evaluating recipes.

I am especially indebted to my colleague Deborah Madison, who styled my food so evocatively; to the extraordinarily talented Laurie Smith, whose mouthwatering pictures illustrate the recipes; as well as to the creative team at Chronicle Books, my editors Bill LeBlond and Sarah Putman, senior designer Laura Lovett, and publicist Mary Ann Gilderbloom.

My agent, Julie Castiglia, I thank for helping turn my idea into reality. Most of all, I am grateful to my husband, Owen, for remaining my biggest fan.

Chokran! Barraka Lla Ofik! Thank you!

Index

Table of Equivalents

The exact equivalents in the following tables have been rounded for convenience.

LIQUID AND DRY MEASURES

U.S.	Metric
1/4 teaspoon	1.25 milliliters
1/2 teaspoon	2.5 milliliters
1 teaspoon	5 milliliters
1 tablespoon (3 teaspoons)	15 milliliters
1 fluid ounce (2 tablespoons)	30 milliliters
1/4 cup	60 milliliters
1/3 cup	80 milliliters
1 cup	240 milliliters
1 pint (2 cups)	480 milliliters
1 quart (4 cups, 32 ounces)	960 milliliters
1 gallon (4 quarts)	3.84 liters
1 ounce (by weight)	28 grams
1 pound	454 grams
2.2 pounds	1 kilogram

OVEN TEMPERATURES

Fahrenheit	Celsius	Gas
250	120	1/2
275	140	1
300	150	2
325	160	3
350	180	4
375	190	5
400	200	6
425	220	7
450	230	8
475	240	9
500	260	10

LENGTH MEASURES

U.S.	Metric
1/8 inch	3 millimeters
1/4 inch	6 millimeters
1/2 inch	12 millimeters
1 inch	2.5 centimeters